Welcome Aboard!

Distinctive cruise music playing (Love Boat theme suggested).

Book Two is exciting and new,
Come aboard, I was expecting you…

For those who have just joined this cruise of veterinary tales, allow me to get you up to speed. There was another book before this, *Cute Poodles, Sweet Old Ladies, and Hugs*. If you're the person who actually read a copy, thanks and welcome back! If you're like everyone else who didn't read it, don't panic, because you can still buy a copy. You can also still read this second book first. That first book then will be like a really cool prequel for you. Good news if you just came aboard, this book will still be funny. However, this book will be even funnier if you read that first one.

As far as what actually goes down in these books, don't worry, I'll explain that too. Have you been on an endless search for that perfect heartwarming animal story? Perhaps you've been looking for stories about what a vet learned from all their loving clients and patients, in order to grow not only as a veterinarian but as a human being. A book of stories so special that its uplifting lessons of love, care, and compassion will transform your life. If so, then keep looking, because this is NOT the book for you. If you happen to have the hard copy in your hands, read it anyway and, who knows, I could be wrong about all that.

This book, however, is another cornucopia of fun-to-read stories depicting what it's *really* like to be a veterinarian. This fun-filled veterinary cruise promises something for (almost) every animal lover. As usual, I've included some unique clients, a couple of touching moments, and brought back my endearing (one is borderline dysfunctional) staff members. So, are you looking to have some fun?

Of course, you are! Then take a stroll up the gangway and come aboard! Trust me. What could possibly go wrong in a book?

Designer Dogs, Awkward Hugs & a Pigeon

Veterinary Tales, Again

By

P.J. Miller, B.V.M.&S., M.R.C.V.S.

Published by thirty8street Publishing

The author's moral rights have been asserted.

ISBN Number 978-0-692-17137-0

Cover design by WordSugar Designs

Dedicated to my wife and children, my staff, and, of course, Jason R. Miller

Contents

That Tuesday

8:32 am (Two Years Ago)

I walked into the treatment area. Jen and Cassey were already getting samples for the annual exams. If I had been one of 'those' veterinary practice owners, I'd have been there earlier. Perhaps even lending a helping hand. I'm not one of those. Truth be told, this works out perfectly, at least for me. They check in the owners and pets for their appointments and get assorted samples, and then I can start the appointments. It's like my cue for a stage show, and my part starts in the exam room. Of course, Jen, our head technician, doesn't see it that way.

"Nice of you to finally get here, Dr. Miller. I drive further than you do and I'm here. What's your excuse this time? Traffic get you again? Don't worry, we got all the hard work done for you already. It's not like YOU got scratched holding that dog. Look at my arm…"

Once she started complaining, I instinctively blocked her out. I had heard it all before. When it comes to giving me a hard time, Jen never lets that opportunity pass her by. I decided to take the high road and refrain from passing judgment on her haircut. She had her black hair cut short to her shoulders, again. That, along with wearing her glasses instead of going with the usual contact lenses, made her a dead ringer for Marcy from the Snoopy cartoons. Jen always hates it when I call her that but I had used that one before and it was getting close to being played out.

So, instead, I headed straight to the fruit arrangement that we'd got yesterday from the Goldbergs. It had just been taken out of the fridge. It was sitting on a counter in the treatment area, seemingly for my enjoyment. I usually wait until after a couple of appointments to start snacking, but after Jen's complaining, I figured I deserved an early chocolate strawberry.

1

I grabbed the patient record sitting in the exam-room door and Cassey led the way with Elwood. Elwood was a hyper five-year-old boxer. Cassey was struggling to hold the end of his leash. Her short, thin stature was no match for him. Her blonde ponytail jumped in rhythmic coordination with each one of Elwood's jerks on the leash. It didn't help matters that he was overly anxious to get back into the exam room with his owner, Mr. Trudeau. Mr. Trudeau was about fifty-something. The remainder of his blonde hair was slicked back, and his skin could not be any darker. He was one of our more *unique* clients. Even though we only saw him once a year, he was definitely one of those clients who stood out. If our practice ever enforced a dress code policy, Mr. Trudeau most likely wouldn't make it in.

He was wearing a bright neon green safety vest, black sweatpants, and work boots. His fashion faux pas on this visit was the thin plastic safety vest that represented the only garment on his torso. His hairy blond chest was exposed and accented by a gold chain that held a small medallion of some sort. Mr. Trudeau is always nice to us but he is always short and to the point. Because of his self-appointed dress code standards, large frame, and matter of fact tone, he gives the impression that he is a person that you don't want to upset. Further complicating things, you really never know if he is joking. This makes almost any situation awkward. Luckily, Elwood remains healthy or is never seriously ill enough that Mr. Trudeau thinks we need to see him. We only see Elwood for his annual exams.

"Hey, Doc, how's it going? Looks like Elwood is ready to get out of here. He thinks he's all done," he said letting out a laugh. Mr. Trudeau was sitting on the exam-room bench with his back straight, his legs slightly apart, and his left hand on his knee supporting his upper body. Had he been wearing a suit and tie instead of his normal attire, his perfect posture and intense facial expression would make him look like he was a businessman ready to close that big deal. That image, of course, fell apart, as the neon safety vest left little to the imagination, putting his tanned hairy chest and pot belly on full display. Cassey knelt down next to Elwood, holding him, as I started my physical exam.

"Elwood looks like he's doing well. Any changes with Elwood you want to talk to me about? Any lumps or bumps you may have noticed?" I asked as I finished up my exam.

"No, Doc. What you see is what you get. He's doing great. He did sneak some BBQ last week… well, actually, I gave him a small piece. He had a soft…yellow, you know… number twos for a few days, but then it was back to normal. I know, I know, what you are going to say about table food. But Elwood is my buddy. Hard to resist that cute face. Right, Cassey?" He leaned forward in his seat and then hit her arm with the back of his hand. She let out a laugh in response. I didn't know if she saw the humor in it or, like the rest of the staff, would laugh at any joke he made to avoid any potential conflict.

"You're playing with fire, man, especially with a boxer. They're prone to upset stomach—"

Just then, Jen knocked and then leaned partially through the exam-room door. My staff never interrupt an appointment unless there is a real problem so, I already knew it was something serious. Even before I heard *that* name.

"Dr. Miller, sorry to interrupt but we have an emergency here."

I excused myself and, as I left, I overheard Mr. Trudeau (not so) jokingly say to Cassey, "Looks like I dodged the bullet on that boring lecture." I heard Cassey let out a polite laugh, as the door closed behind me.

"Dr. Miller, you ready for this one?" Jen asked sarcastically, holding the record in her hand. I could read the name on it. She already knew the answer to that question. I was not ready. No one would be ready for that record. In fact, anything associated with this particular name is bad news. Medical cases, phone messages, and even simple prescription refills, they're all bad. If it bears the name Esposito and you're involved, your day just got dumped on.

I'd be the first to tell you that Mrs. Esposito is a really nice person. If you met her or talked with her for any length of time you'd think she was a sweet lady. She'd probably remind you of a favorite aunt, or really cool grandma. You'd think my staff and I were all cruel and most likely burned out dealing with the general public. Don't worry, she fooled all of us too when we first met her. We all figured it out eventually. Even Liz, who was the last hold-out to come around, tried to avoid anything with the Esposito name on it.

I'd first met Ann Marie Esposito five years previously when JJ was a puppy. She had just purchased him from a not-so-reputable source: "A friend of my sister's, who is a 'specialty' breeder." She let us know he was the last one of a sold-out litter, and they *let* her buy him only as a favor to her sister. When Liz was checking her in, that first day, she told her he was a purebred Jack-A-Poo (a Jack Russell-poodle cross). Mrs. Esposito made certain that Liz's spelling matched what was written on her little yellow notepad. If you were really good at reading people, better than we were, that little pad would have been the first clue.

Jack-A-Poo is not what we veterinary professionals consider a pure breed. By that, I mean, recognized by the American Kennel Club (AKC). As far as I am concerned, the AKC is THE authority on what is an official dog breed and what isn't. In other words, if the breed can't qualify to be shown at the big dog show in Madison Square Garden, it's not an official breed. That doesn't mean I'm some kind of dog snob and I only like purebreds. No, I am opposed to people selling 'designer' breeds, especially for high prices. There's no breed standard across the board on these breeds, and many of them are often quite different. From my standpoint, it would be better to adopt a dog that resembled the mix of breeds one had in mind.

As for Mrs. Esposito, she won us over (fooled us good) on that first visit. Like our other clients who fall in the designer-dog/fake-breed trap, we gave her a pass. She was engaging and open to all our recommendations. It was also obvious she had a strong love for JJ.

JJ was friendly and tried to lick us no matter what procedure we were doing. He never changed and was the model patient. He resembles almost every other Jack Russell-mix dog I've seen, and we have never been able to recognize any of the supposed special poodle components in him. He has a white wiry coat, with light brown spots, including a distinctive brown spot around his right eye.

I confess, I also got suckered in. I had an affinity for Mrs. Esposito because she was from New York City (Queens). And since I am from New York City, I have a bias toward New Yorkers. Most, unfortunately not all, New Yorkers turn out to be tremendous clients in my practice. The others that turn out to be not-so-tremendous, do so on their own. At which time, Jen will be sure to highlight the fact that another one of *my favorite New York clients* has either jumped ship or was kicked out. Eventually, Mrs. Esposito became another example of one of my prestigious New Yorker clients that Jen still likes to use against me.

Over the next few years, Mrs. Esposito's visits became more frequent, and it wasn't because JJ was actually sick. Since animals can't tell us their issues, it becomes crucial to get accurate information from their owners. For the record, I don't think my clients are all hypochondriacs. Actually, I usually go by the complete opposite assumption. Most clients are very astute about what is going on with their pet. I cannot tell you how many times I have diagnosed a problem because a client thought something wasn't 'right' with their pet. The signs may not have been medically obvious at first but their instinct was correct. Unfortunately, Mrs. Esposito wasn't one of those clients.

Believe it or not, Munchausen syndrome by proxy has been proven to occur in veterinary medicine. In that condition, a caregiver fabricates, exaggerates, or induces mental or physical health problems in those who are in their care. They do this, in order to get attention or sympathy. I don't believe she had that particular syndrome but

5

whatever she started doing wasn't too healthy for our mental well-being. The majority of the time, when she called us with a concern or came in with JJ, it wasn't a real medical problem. If it was a problem, she would blow it way out of proportion. Over the next few years, the concerns, comprehensive yellow-pad notes, and supposed illnesses seemed to multiply.

There were many of these instances but one of the most memorable was when she came in because she thought that JJ was having seizures. She had read up about epilepsy in dogs online and had already diagnosed him with it. Her yellow notepad was filled with questions about epilepsy and treatment options. This made getting information from her even more difficult because I couldn't figure out if she was applying what she'd read online or describing the real signs that JJ was having.

As with several previous illnesses, JJ's tests came back completely normal. I ruled out a lot of other potential causes of seizures with normal blood work. But on that occasion, I outed her with an even more modern and advantageous veterinary instrument; her cell phone. I asked her to record JJ's episodes with a video on her phone. The next day when she returned to go over his blood work, she was excited that she had captured not one but three of these seizure-type episodes.

"Dr. Millah, I'm not crazy! And JJ does have epilepsy."

I am only qualified to definitely respond to the last statement and I can tell that JJ is not an epileptic. It took me ten minutes to explain away the episodes. The first two—really one incident recorded over two clips—were of him rolling on the floor with excitement. The third was him happily rolling on his back in the grass sunning himself. I got her to promise she wouldn't worry any longer about epilepsy or record any more videos.

It took forty-eight hours for her to break that promise and return with a video to show Liz, of him doing laps in her living room. Liz was able to talk her out of another appointment. For reasons unknown to me,

Liz's second opinion apparently was the confirmation she was looking for and she never recorded any more videos after that.

On *that* Tuesday morning, Mrs. Esposito ran into the practice and straight into an exam room. She was cradling JJ in her arms like a baby. Liz, thinking it might be a real emergency, left the front desk and ran in behind her. Mrs. Esposito immediately took a seat on the bench. She started rocking back and forth with JJ.

In her thick New York accent, she stammered, "We need Dr. Millah. JJ has been spittin' up all night. This mornin' he's lifeless...lifeless!"

Liz saw that JJ was a bit lethargic but he was still wagging his tail even in her arms. She immediately knew it wasn't the dire emergency that Mrs. Esposito made it out to be.

"It will just be a couple of minutes, Mrs. Esposito. I'll get Dr. Miller." Liz got his record and went to the treatment area to fill Jen in. As soon as Liz got done explaining things to Jen, Mrs. Esposito let out a muffled cry from behind the exam-room door.

"Liz, puh-lease, hurry! Don't leave us hangin'." After hearing that, Jen thought it would be a good time to get me out of the exam room with Mr. Trudeau and put an end to this situation sooner rather than later.

I went into the exam room and Mrs. Esposito was wearing her classic attire. There are several clients in our practice who seem to wear a trademark outfit every time we see them, almost like a uniform. Mrs. Esposito was definitely one of those. She was wearing her patented white golf visor, velour tracksuit, and white sneakers. That day, the tracksuit was dark purple. She had (dyed) red, curly hair that reached her shoulders. She was a tiny woman, a few inches over five feet, and my best guess puts her in her late sixties.

"Thank Gawd, Dr. Millah, are we glad to see you! JJ is not doin' well. He must have spit up five times last night. I was up all night with him, wipin' his little face. Then, this mornin', he's not eatin' and he's

7

layin' around. It's like he can't walk. I rushed right over. I knew you would want to see him."

By the way, spit up is what many owners call vomiting. They think by downgrading it to spit up, it will make it less serious. Despite usually exaggerating everything else, Mrs. Esposito still calls vomiting spit up. I already knew getting an accurate medical history from Mrs. Esposito would be close to impossible. Not only does she embellish clinical signs but she will also throw in extraneous information.

"How many times has he vomited in the last twenty-four hours?"

"He's not vomiting. It's only spit up. After he spit up the first couple of times, I got worried. So, I started giving him Peedio-lyte with a syringe, so he wouldn't get dehydrated. I have to go to the Walgreens by the park to get it 'cause the one near me stopped carrying the grape flavor. He seems to like grape the best. Dr. Millah, I can't tell you how many times that Peedio-lyte has saved him when he got sick. When he spit it all up at six this morning is when I started to get *really* worried."

I don't advocate giving pets Pedialyte. I had also shared this opinion with Mrs. Esposito more than once. The last time, it looked like she had written my advice directly on her pad. I was convinced then that I had seen the end of the grape 'Peedio-lyte.'

I never got an exact, or even close to accurate, number on the vomiting. The rest of the history (information about the sick pet) was also all over the place. I desperately tried to keep Mrs. Esposito on point but it was useless. After my last question, she started a whole conversation on an old-school remedy from her Italian grandmother.

The story was non-stop and I was only able to interrupt her in order to let her know we'd be taking blood from JJ. The story was so long that I did my exam, Jen left, got JJ's blood, brought him back, and she still wasn't finished. After Jen left for the second time, to run JJ's blood work, Mrs. Esposito dropped a bomb on me out of nowhere.

"I'm surprised he is able to walk OK now. He could barely walk this morning. His hind legs were really wobbly, almost like he was draggin' 'em all around da house."

After she said that, I looked down at JJ, who Jen had placed on the floor. Usually, Mrs. Esposito would've scooped him back into her arms but she was so focused on our conversation she had let him wander the exam room. I watched him carefully and he was walking fine but did seem to have a slight limp on his right rear leg. In Mrs. Esposito's defense, this happens all the time. Owners will bring something else up or ask me to check something else conveniently after the tech has left the exam room. Making matters worse, Cassey was nowhere to be found so I had to ask Jen.

"Dr. Miller, why don't you do a complete physical exam the first time? It would save me a lot of time having to go back in for a second exam. This is going to be the last time, right? You better make sure she doesn't invent any more signs after this 'cause I'm not going into that room again." She finished her statement right before we opened the door to the exam room. Jen was already having doubts about whether there was actually anything seriously wrong with JJ.

Despite her objections, Jen was a more than willing participant. I knew she was anxious to find out if anything was really wrong with JJ. Jen, like all of us, had an affinity for the little dog. But, for reasons I could never really figure out, she also had a bizarre affinity toward Mrs. Esposito. It wasn't obvious to me at first. Later, though, I noticed it was always Jen who picked up the on-holds for Mrs. Esposito. She also spent ages on the phone with her, and without fail, seemed to linger in the exam room with her long after I was gone.

Jen placed JJ on the table. I thoroughly, at least this time, carried out his orthopedic exam. I manipulated both his hind legs and hips; he never showed any signs of pain or discomfort. I even manipulated his head and neck and palpated along his back and still nothing. Everything appeared normal. In fact, he started to become more animated after my exam. When Jen placed him on the floor he started

9

racing around the exam room and even jumped up into Mrs. Esposito's lap.

"I know you think I'm crazy but he couldn't walk this morning. He acts like he's fine now but something ain't right. He's sick. I know he is."

"Aside from the problems with his back legs, and vomiting, anything else, at all…. anything that's …abnormal?" I asked trying to finalize his list of problems (real or otherwise), especially before Jen bailed out of the room. It wouldn't have mattered anyway because before she could answer Jen was gone.

"No. Aside from not eating this morning, that's it."

"Well, let's see what his blood work shows and then we can come up with a game plan," I said as I excused myself and left the exam room.

Jen was just outside, in the lab area waiting for the lab machine's printer to finalize his results. She noticed me inching closer, anxious to see if I'd get any info from his lab work, even though we both knew the answer.

"I don't know what you're expecting to find, Dr. Miller. You know it's going to be normal. She probably slipped him table food and he's got an upset stomach. You think she tells you everything she gives him? I'll be the one who has to call and check on him tomorrow and she'll confess it to me, you watch." Just as she finished, she took the paper from the printer and handed it to me. Spoiling the surprise of his results she stated, "Normal. What did I tell you?"

She continued, "Treat it and street it! Let us know what you want for this dog. Cassey has got the next appointment to check it in," Jen stated, motioning to Cassey who had just walked in from the door to the kennel area.

The ball was now officially in Dr. Miller's court. My biggest worry would be missing a potential diagnosis. Was Mrs. Esposito crying wolf again with JJ? I didn't want to be negligent. I also didn't want to go down the Mrs. Esposito hole and run a bunch of unnecessary tests, chasing down signs that didn't even exist. I quickly dismissed any thoughts of a serious medical problem. I started thinking maybe Jen knew something I didn't. Maybe her bizarre relationship with Mrs. Esposito had given her inside information that Mrs. Esposito occasionally slipped JJ table food. Table food is the most common cause of a simple upset stomach and pancreatitis. Both of which could explain the vomiting.

I went back in the room with JJ's lab work. I slid it across the exam table to show it to Mrs. Esposito. I explained to her it was normal, and that we had enough blood to send to the outside lab to run a test for pancreatitis. The normal blood work had set her mind at ease that nothing was seriously wrong with JJ. Since JJ had walked around the room, and jumped up into her lap, even she was ready to overlook the slight limp as a serious medical problem. I went over the treatment plan ('treat him and street him' protocol). I told her we would give JJ subcutaneous fluids, an injection for the vomiting, and some narcotic tablets for pain. I explained to her it would cover his slight limp, and any abdominal pain if he had pancreatitis. I knew she would never admit, at least to me, that she gave JJ any table food but, at that point, I was convinced she had slipped him something.

I was wrong. My diagnosis wasn't even in the same neighborhood as JJ's real problem. But even if I had been medically paranoid, there was no test or medical plan I could have performed to diagnose or help JJ at that point. It turned out to be one of the most bizarre presentations of a relatively common problem I had ever seen in private practice. Mrs. Esposito would be back with JJ with a very real problem, and every ounce of worry would be justified.

Mrs. Esposito left, but not after talking to Jen in the exam room for over ten minutes. When Jen came out I confronted her. I reprimanded her for taking too long to discharge Mrs. Esposito. Reprimanding Jen at my hospital is exactly like when any stereotypical sassy, head nurse gets reprimanded on TV. It does no good. They usually have some funny comeback that only makes the doctor (patsy) look worse for opening their mouth in the first place.

I have been working with Jen for over fifteen years and I'd learned this a long time ago. So, because of this, I chose my reprimands carefully. In this particular case, I was trying to get lucky that her comeback would involve a table food confession from Mrs. Esposito. I figured it would be worth it. It wasn't.

"Dr. Miller, it's not my fault that you can't explain stuff clearly so that she can understand it. Some of these people need my touch, to lay it out nice and simple for them. I put their mind at ease. By now, you, of all people, should know that Mrs. Esposito is one of those people. Is it my fault that out of everyone in this hospital, she picks me to latch on to? Do you think I like that job? You're welcome, by the way. I straightened it *all* out for you. She told me to thank you but you should be thanking me."

I didn't give Jen the 'thank you' she was looking for. Instead, I deflected and complained about having to check in the cat appointment with Cassey, which left me to do the tech work and to get all the samples myself. As expected, she failed to feel sorry for me replying, "It's about time you pitch in and do some real work around here."

Just then, we heard Mrs. Esposito scream out from the reception area. "He can't walk. He's paralyzed! Oh my Gawd, Liz!" The rest of the conversation was muffled. At first, I didn't believe what I was hearing. There is no way there could be anything wrong with JJ. I had just seen him less than thirty minutes ago.

That Tuesday, Part II

10:10 am

Liz led Mrs. Esposito back into the same exam room, just like she had earlier. This time, Mrs. Esposito was crying, and visibly shaking. She was trying to talk but exactly what she was trying to say was incoherent because of her sobbing. Liz took command of the situation. She knew despite whatever was or wasn't going on, I was the immediate solution.

"Don't worry, Mrs. Esposito, Dr. Miller will be right in!"

Jen and I had instinctively gathered outside the exam-room door. Liz handed off the record to me, saying only, "They both don't look too good if you ask me." She then, instantly, hurried back up front to answer the phone and left us to draw our own conclusions.

I didn't know if Liz believed there was anything wrong with JJ or was trying to hedge her bets with that vague comment but, at that point, it didn't matter. I was convinced that he was probably fine and that this time Mrs. Esposito had crossed the line. When Jen and I walked into the exam room, Mrs. Esposito was still sobbing uncontrollably, and cradling JJ in her arms. This time she stood up and placed JJ on the exam table immediately, to show us what was wrong.

As soon as Jen and I saw him on the exam table we both knew she wasn't inventing any signs this time. Any feeling of anger and frustration I'd had, quickly dissipated. I instantly became concerned and genuinely worried. A wave of guilt came over me for thinking she had made this all up and for potentially missing it earlier. I was confused by what I was seeing him. My brain had difficulty processing the information since I expected him to be completely normal. The fact that none of this was remotely apparent when I had seen him didn't matter. The second-guessing in my mind had already all begun.

On the exam table, JJ was hopelessly trying to propel himself forward with his front legs. His back legs splayed out behind him like a frog and dangled behind him like useless appendages. It was as if he was trying to come to grips with the fact his back legs were no longer working. Mrs. Esposito wasn't exaggerating this time. She was right, and his signs were obvious.

Jen's mood, like mine, also palpably changed to concern. She slid in next to Mrs. Esposito and prevented JJ from scooting any further. Mrs. Esposito took a step off to the side and produced a wad of tissues from her warm-up suit-jacket pocket and blew her nose. After which she stammered, "I don't, don't understand. He was fine when I got home. Just like you guys saw him here. I put him in his bed to rest. I didn't even have a chance to give him the pills. Then the doorbell rang…he got up to run…and then just collapsed…what, what happened to him? Could, the injection… have, have, done dis?"

"No. This isn't a possible side effect from the injection," I blankly stated, as I started re-examining JJ. I repeated his physical exam and it was normal. I knew the information I was looking for would come from his neurologic exam. In my mind, I was still second-guessing myself for missing all this earlier and wasn't taking any chances. His basic physical exam was normal, aside from the obvious neurologic abnormalities. I then tried to focus on his neurologic exam as Mrs. Esposito continued to fire questions at me.

"Does he have… men-un-gitis? Could that be it?"

"I don't think that's what's going on—."

Just then, JJ let out a high-pitched bark as I pressed along his middle back. Mrs. Esposito let out a scream of her own in response to JJ's. After which she inhaled dramatically as if she was holding her breath, and then took her wad of tissues and held them up to her face.

She restarted her sobbing at an even higher level than before. No pet owner wants to see their baby in pain and, even though Mrs. Esposito's response may have been more dramatic than most, it was

14

understandable given JJ's situation. Appearing to be in a brief state of shock, she paused briefly from asking any more questions and tried to gather herself together. I took the opportunity to focus on my exam, uninterrupted, and confirm my tentative diagnosis on JJ.

His primary problem was that his hind legs had severe neurologic deficits but they were not paralyzed. His front legs, just like the rest of his neurologic exam, were normal. I suspected he had a 'slipped disk' in his back. Just like in people, dogs have spongy cushions in between their vertebrae. If they get damaged, swollen, or if they rupture, they can compress the nerves in the spinal cord. When this happens, the nerve pathways (messages to and from the brain) are interrupted resulting in neurological deficits. The vomiting was an entirely different matter, and at this point, I suspected, unrelated to his main, and most important problem.

I finished his exam and started to make a few quick notes on his record. Before I could start explaining the situation, Mrs. Esposito recovered and anxiously asked, "What's wrong with my baby? Are you going to be able to help him?" She was still holding the tissues in front of her face, which slightly muffled her question.

I went on to explain what was going on with his back. I also told her I thought it was unrelated to his vomiting and that I wasn't able to tie the two together. Since his back was the most obvious and distressing problem, I was able to get her to focus on that and forget about the vomiting. Explaining all that was the easy part. The hard part was about to come next. I knew that would be a challenge but I had no idea on how truly difficult it really was going to be.

So difficult, in fact, that if this particular case is even mentioned in our practice, Jen will cut off that person with, "Stop! I don't ever want to hear about that again. Understand!? Are you trying to give me diarrhea?" The latter part of her statement referring to any stress that is so severe, it adversely affects her bowel. A fact that she has no problem openly sharing whenever the situation arises.

15

"Mrs. Esposito, ideally, the plan would be to refer him to our local veterinary specialist neurologists. They would be able to give us a second opinion. Most likely, perform an MRI of his back. If it's confirmed that he has a significant disk issue, then the treatment would be surgery—"

"I don't know about taking him anywhere else right now. He is in a lot of pain. I'd rather not drive him anywhere. I'd rather just leave him here for you guys to fix him."

"Mrs. Esposito, there is a chance that the only way to fix his problem is with surgery. To find out, we need to have him seen at a specialist. If that's his problem, the quicker he is seen the better. I know it can be expensive, especially if they end up taking him to surgery. If you want I can call them and get an estimate for you…" The money issue is always a no-win situation but it has to be discussed. Regardless, I always feel like an ass, one way or another, for even having to bring it up.

"It's not the money, Dr. Millah, you know JJ is my baby. I would do whatever it takes for him. It's all just…just so confusing. I don't want to drive that far with him. It's too far. I know he needs to go, I guess…"

She paused, in what seemed like an eternity, as she wiped her nose and replaced the wad of tissues back into her pocket. I wanted to make sure she was done speaking before restarting. Jen made it feel even longer.

Jen started displaying her 'greatest hits' of facial gestures in an effort to get this referral underway. In case you were wondering, the specialist is a thirty-minute drive from our practice. Mrs. Esposito is more than enough of a competent driver to make the trip. I couldn't wait any longer for her to continue. When Jen looked down at her watch as a final dig to push this along, I restarted.

"Mrs. Esposito, it's only thirty minutes. Don't worry, I am also going to give JJ an injection for his pain. He'll be comfortable for the ride. You'll be fine."

16

"I don't know. I just don't know what to do, at this point..."

I decided it was time to take control of the situation. I had been at these crossroads many times with other clients. In this particular case, I had no doubts that Mrs. Esposito would do anything for JJ regardless of cost. However, despite what clients tell us regarding finances, it's our standard protocol, as well as courtesy, to call ahead and get them an estimate. This way they are kept abreast of what to expect at the specialist, and there is no unnecessary 'sticker shock' over the care of their pet.

"Mrs. Esposito, we are going to take JJ back and get his pain medication on board. He can hang out in a kennel in the treatment area. I am going to call the neurologists and get you an estimate." Before I could finish, Jen, anxious to leave, scooped up JJ and brushed past behind me to the treatment area. As I turned to leave, Mrs. Esposito slumped down on the exam bench exhausted.

When Jen and I returned to the treatment area with JJ, Jen was in full effect. She glanced over to my next appointment's record sitting in the holder on the other exam's room door.

"Let's get this going, Dr. Miller. Your next appointment is here already. That's Mr. Deny, and you know what that cat is like. The longer it waits, the more pissed it's going to get. So, let's get this referral going. You know I'm only looking out for you."

Cassey got up the narcotic injection almost instantly after I gave her the dose. As she gave it, I picked up the phone and called down to the neurologist. I stared at JJ who was calmly resting in the cage, even though it would be several minutes before the drug took effect.

Even over the phone they already suspected that he most likely had a disk issue that would require surgery. The estimate was a big number, one with three zeros after it. They ended the call telling me to give them a heads up if, and when, JJ would be on the way. I was on my way back to go into the exam room when Jen stopped me.

"Don't do it, Dr. Miller. Don't go back in that room. Do this appointment. It will be quick and then you can go and talk to her. You'll never get out of there."

I ignored her and went back in to talk to Mrs. Esposito. I was actually on the fence on doing the other appointment first. Sometimes, I get into the trouble doing the opposite of what Jen recommends. In an effort to try to show her who the boss really is, or out of spite, I won't listen. As an added bonus, if the opposing way works out, I'll use it against her later on. This was not going to be one of those times.

"OK, Mrs. Esposito, we gave JJ the narcotic injection. I spoke to the specialist, and they also suspect that it is, in fact, a disk problem that might need surgery," I explained and then added in the cost.

"The money is not the problem, Dr. Millah, not for JJ. I just don't know if I want to take him there and put him through all that." She didn't even lift her head. I could barely see her eyes under the white golf visor, with her sitting on the bench.

"He'll be fine. I had a similar surgery done on my bulldog a while back. He did great. The biggest problem was keeping him confined after surgery." I thought that this answer would put her mind at ease, it didn't. As soon as I heard her next question, I knew I was going to be stuck in that exam room just as Jen had predicted. I also knew Jen would not miss the opportunity, later on, to remind me of that.

"You said, he *might* need surgery. So, what would they do if he didn't need surgery?"

"Well, first, it could be something entirely different, in which case the treatment would be different. But some cases, which aren't as severe, can sometimes be treated with steroids, pain medication, and strict rest. We do that sometimes in a Plan-B scenario, like when owners, unfortunately, can't afford the specialist."

"Can we do that for JJ and I'll just leave him here for a few days?"

18

"We could but, if he does need surgery, it won't work. Also, waiting could potentially make things worse and affect his prognosis."

The back and forth went on for about another ten minutes. She finally relented, and reluctantly agreed. I told her we would make copies of JJ's records and Cassey would carry JJ to the car. As I left the exam room, Jen was waiting right outside the door.

"What did I tell you, Dr. Miller? I hope you're happy. You can hear that cat growling through the door. Nice! Did you think he'd get better, waiting in there all this time? Cassey will deal with all that. Let's go!" she said, motioning to the exam room.

She handed me the record. She was already prepared and anxiously waiting. She had the Kevlar safety gloves, used for cats like cats like this one, under her arm and the vaccines in her hand. She led the way into the exam room, and her mood instantly changed like she'd flipped a switch. Jen was talented that way, and never let situations dictate her mood in the exam room. In the rest of the hospital, we weren't always as fortunate with where that switch was positioned.

"Hey, Mr. Deny, how are we doing today? How's good old Johnny doing?" she said jovially greeting them and trying to downplay the impending disaster we were about to experience known as Johnny Cash Deny.

"He's pissed off!" Mr. Deny replied without missing a beat. Hugh Deny was sitting on the exam-room bench. He was wearing black dress pants, black Velcro sneakers, white socks, and a button-down short-sleeve red plaid shirt. He was bald but grew his (dyed) jet black hair long on the sides so he could comb it over the top. He had black thick-rimmed glasses, and my guess would put him in his late seventies. Unfortunately, like his cat, Johnny Cash, he is also overweight.

Mr. Deny represents the classic grumpy old man. Most, if not all my recommendations remain unanswered. They also always elicit some sort of wisecrack. Having said that, in the last seven years I've known

19

Mr. Deny, I've come to realize that this is all just part of his rough Detroit exterior. Sometimes, I think it's all just an act that amuses him, playing the part of the cranky old man.

I've actually caught him being overly polite and friendly with the staff on several occasions. He even insists on giving the tech that helps him to the car a tip, which is usually at least a ten-dollar bill. Of course, he always says, "I know that cheap ass Dr. Miller probably pays like crap. Here, take this. You deserve it." I don't know if he's joking or not but, for the record, my staff get paid well enough not to require supplementary handouts.

Jen put on the Kevlar gloves and started getting Johnny out of the cat carrier as it sat on the exam table. I tried to make small talk with Mr. Deny but that was as difficult as getting Johnny out of the carrier. Jen had her work cut out for her because Johnny could barely fit through the door of it. Add in the Kevlar gloves, as well as him backing up and resisting her every move, and it was nearly impossible.

Jen's talented, and despite his protesting, she negotiated him out of the carrier. He was growling loudly as she placed him on the scale. I put the carrier under the table. The massive, all-white three-year-old cat, tipped the scale at nineteen pounds. He probably should have weighed about thirteen. As soon as Jen quietly said the weight, Mr. Deny asked, "What did he weigh last year?!"

"Eighteen," I reluctantly replied.

"Oh well, it is what it is. I can tell you that cat is never going to lose weight. So, Doc, you can save that stale, old, crap lecture. I know he's fat. Who isn't? At least he gets to enjoy life. My doctor tries to tell me the same crap. I'm still here, and no medication either."

I don't know if he's lucky enough to not be on any medication. More than likely, however, his doctor got the same directions on where he could put his prescriptions as Mr. Deny gave me with the flea prevention I'd told him about.

Jen expertly held Johnny, despite his growling and repeated attempts to swat and bite me during the exam. The whole time she whispered to him like he was a loving pet, instead of a fractious cat. I finished my brief exam, which, of course, omitted the rectal temperature. Sticking anything in Johnny's backside is just asking for trouble. I then gave him his vaccines. After the last one, he let out a blood-curdling scream and then exploded with rage. The byproduct having to do more with his behavior than any pain from a simple subcutaneous vaccination.

Our time had run out with Johnny, and he was now gator rolling and trying to break free of Jen's hold. I instinctively grabbed the carrier. I held it up with its back on the floor, while Jen placed him in it and let gravity do all the work. As I closed the door, he swatted at me through the bars and scratched the back of my hand.

"Don't feel bad, Jen. I know he likes you. He likes you a lot. Things would be a lot different if it was just you. It's only because you have to hold him for Dr. Miller. That's why he's like that. I know for a fact he doesn't like Dr. Miller," he said winking at Jen and smiling. "You OK, Doc?" he asked, breaking character for a brief moment.

"I'm fine. It's just a small scratch," I replied wiping the blood off with a paper hand towel.

"Yeah, he was just warning you. If he wanted, he'd take the whole hand. It looks like he left you a little present on the table, Doc..." he said pointing to the small turd that Johnny had left on the exam table during his struggle. "That's for Dr. Miller. That's what he thinks of your place here," he said, chuckling at his own joke.

"Don't worry, Mr. Deny. We can actually use that as his stool sample," I replied. That's how we check for intestinal parasites.

"That's good, 'cause I wasn't going to bring you one," Mr. Deny replied as he started to get up. Jen grabbed his carrier and volunteered to help him out to the car. He slowly and deliberately got up out of his seat and started to shuffle out of the exam room as Jen opened the door in front of him. Despite his boasting about his health, it was obvious

21

that going anywhere was becoming difficult for Mr. Deny. He had aged dramatically in the last few years.

As he walked through the door, he turned to me, and said, "I'll see what I can do with the weight but I'm not promising nothing. Sorry about the scratch. But let's face it, you deserve it for those shots you gave him." He then smiled, winked at me, and left.

I went back to the treatment area expecting to find Mrs. Esposito gone but, instead, I saw Cassey walking out of the exam room saying, "Dr. Miller will be back in, in a minute." I glanced over and JJ was still in the kennel. I walked over to Cassey and, before I could ask, she sheepishly explained, "Mrs. Esposito has a few more questions for you? She's not sure now if she is going to the specialist. She wants to talk about... about other options..."

I wanted to start arguing with Cassey as if she had messed it all up while I was in the other exam room. I knew it wasn't her fault so, I caught myself before saying anything. I'm not always that lucky. I have got into trouble opening my mouth without thinking before.

I was beyond frustrated. I can deal with Plan B when the specialist is not an option but dealing with Mrs. Esposito's indecision, or whatever she was obsessing about, is an entirely different situation.

I turned and quickly went back into the exam room. This time she was standing. She was leaning on the exam table. She had 'broken out' the little yellow pad from her purse. The top page was filled with notes. As I entered the room, she stated, "We need to talk."

Her tone had changed. She was now more composed. She acted as if I had either given her misleading information or not enough information for her to make an informed decision. She made me start from the beginning and explain everything: the disk, the MRI, the surgery, the qualifications of the specialist, all of it. It was obvious from the questions she was asking that she had absorbed it all and that her previous emotional state had nothing to do with her desire to get the information all over again.

I felt like I was being interrogated and that all my statements were going on the Esposito record. I could only hope she was accurately transcribing what I was saying on the little yellow pad. I was also hoping she wouldn't misinterpret those scribbled notes later on. It's a given that clients often misinterpret what I say to family members. I am used to that. I was worried that some sort of misinformation would be directly relayed from that pad to the specialist and their staff. I'd look like some worthless incompetent vet. Then later, that would serve to ignite a storm of rumors and gossip at the specialists. From then on, I'd be branded as, "You know, *that* Dr. Miller."

After multiple questions and a full two pages of notes she looked up and asked her last question, "Dr. Millah, is it OK if I call my sistah real quick?" She took her phone out of her pocket. She covered the phone and held it to her chest as if her sister was already on the line and she was preventing her from hearing our conversation. She then stared at me intently and I knew this was my cue to take a break from the interrogation.

As soon as I walked outside the room, Jen had long returned from helping Mr. Deny and was waiting outside. Just as I had shifted the blame onto Cassey, Jen had now shifted the blame onto me. Except she didn't hold back from arguing with me.

"I don't know why you had to start talking to her about medication to treat a disk. Had you gone into the exam room *when* I told you, you wouldn't have been scratched, Mrs. Esposito would be on the way to the specialist, and we'd all be having lunch. Tell me, am I right, Dr. Miller?"

I was trying to craft the perfect response for Jen. Even though she may have been right about the Johnny Cash appointment, I wasn't going to admit it. I wasn't about to take the fall for this one either. Mrs. Esposito would still be here regardless if I had gone in that exam room.

Just then Mrs. Esposito knocked on the exam-room door and then poked her head out into the treatment area. She held the phone to her chest, looked at Jen and said, "Jen, could you do me a favah? Could you tawlk to my sistah for a second? You are so very good at makin' all this stuff so simple."

Even Jen was confused by this request. It's quite a regular occurrence for me to get dragged into cell phone conversations with family members, even if they don't actually live with the owner. This was a first for Jen. It didn't matter, Jen nonchalantly took the cell phone and then back into the exam room they both went to start their little conference.

Cassey and I gave each other confused looks. She just shrugged her shoulders and didn't say a word, trying to hear what was being discussed in the exam room. It's not uncommon for clients in our practice to latch on to certain staff members. In our practice, if this happens, it's inevitably Liz. That staff member then becomes the focal point for every interaction and question. As long as she agrees with the treatment, specific medication, or recommendation then it must be the right thing to do.

In Mrs. Esposito's case, she'd get the occasional second opinion from Liz but she was latched on to Jen. Another veterinarian or new grad might be upset by this scenario. It could be conceived as a form of client mistrust and a huge blow to one's ego. Not for me. They may be putting their own spin on it but they're just repeating what I've already said.

In this case, I was actually relieved I didn't have to talk to the sister and explain it all a third time. I was also starting to take pleasure in the fact that I could give a Jen hard time about this bizarre relationship yet again. I was starting to gather quotes from excerpts I heard through the door, that I could then repeat to Jen later on. Of course, as you'll see, that turned out to be a waste of time.

Within a few minutes, Jen victoriously emerged from the exam room. She boldly told Cassey to give Mrs. Esposito copies of her records and blood work. She then went to the kennel and got JJ. As she went into the exam room, she said, "Don't worry, Mrs. Esposito. I'll help you to

24

the car with JJ. Dr. Miller will phone and let them know you're on the way."

As the door was closing, Mrs. Esposito caught a glimpse of me, waved and said, "Thanks, Dr. Millah, for everything. I feel so much better now."

To me, it felt more as if I was an observer on the sidelines. I was a bit player with just a minor supporting role. It was a thank you in passing, and the real star was Jen. It was quiet for a few moments with Jen and Cassey both helping Mr. Esposito in the parking lot. I called the specialist and told them JJ was on the way.

I was finishing writing up JJ's record when Jen came back into the treatment area. It was then that I realized any premium highlights I had gathered from her little conference were absolutely useless.

"I just have one thing to say, Dr. Miller. What would you do without me guiding these people?"

I already knew it wasn't a rhetorical question, and that wasn't going to be the only thing she had to say. It was really just her opening statement.

"You know what I had to do in that room? Trust me, it wasn't fun. I had to be like, like some sort of…liaison! That's it, I'm like a veterinary liaison! You fly in and out of these rooms and give some quick explanation in vet language. These people don't have any idea about what you're saying. Then, I have to go in as the *liaison* and clean things up. You're lucky she loves me. I know how to handle things. I think, really, I probably should be a therapist. I'd be good at it too. Even her sister loves me now. I'm like a vet tech/therapist liaison for these people. If it wasn't for me… Scratch that. If it wasn't for *ALL* of us girls here, you'd be screwed!"

There's some truth in that but I wasn't about to agree with Jen.

One Week Later

JJ did end up having surgery on his back. He did great. The test for pancreatitis came back slightly elevated, and it was later determined or rather confessed to Jen, "That he might have, possibly, got some French fries, I *accidentally* dropped."

After speaking with the specialist, she agreed that his presentation was strange. She thought it might have been a bulging disk that ruptured when he went home. It was still hard to explain him being essentially normal after the owner potentially witnessed him having real issues earlier in the morning. I didn't belabor the point with the specialist because, in the middle of talking to her, I had flashbacks to Mrs. Esposito's pad. For the rest of the phone call, I couldn't tell if she was talking to me as if I was now *THAT* Dr. Miller.

To this day, I have no explanation as to how or why his case transpired the way it did. Any other disk issue I have ever seen has been obvious from the start. I also don't know if Mrs. Esposito's yellow pad 'poisoned the well' with my reputation at the specialist. Since then, every time I'm on the phone with the neurologist I always start thinking back to the yellow pad.

Later that week, Mrs. Esposito did stop by and let us know JJ was back home and doing great. She had many directions on the little yellow pad from the specialist. She made sure to confirm them all with Jen. She also brought us a pound cake with fresh strawberries and a thank-you card.

> *I want to thank you all for the great care and attention.*
> *Especially Jen for helping guide my mom and auntie in making*
> *a very difficult decision. Hope you enjoy my mom's homemade*
> *pound cake. Be sure to share some with my favorite doctor, Dr.*
> *Miller.*
>
> *Love and Kisses,*
> *JJ*

I know what you're thinking about little sweet Mrs. Esposito. Trust me on this one. She didn't last, and it wasn't our fault that time. Really, it wasn't.

The Complete Unabridged Story of "Dude"

My cases aren't always that complicated. One of the simplest cases, if you even want to call it a case, was long before I was even a veterinarian. There was no real client involved but that didn't mean it didn't come along with any drama. Incidentally, this particular story was the source of the essay I used to apply for college. As far as the colleges I applied to were concerned, it was the main reason I wanted to become a veterinarian. It's true, it influenced my decision but I had already decided I was going to be a veterinarian long before Dude. So, maybe that part was a slight embellishment.

The story, however, is true. In fact, I had to simplify it, shorten it, and water it down (make it politically correct) for the essay. I am pretty sure they still liked it. I did get in to most of the universities I applied to. I know for a fact my high school English teacher loved it. They all liked it, and they didn't even get the entire story with all the details.

It all happened when I was fifteen. I was hanging out with my friend, Jason Miller. You could call him my best friend but, like all lifelong friends, his job description goes way beyond that. We grew up in the same apartment building in Manhattan, and he lived two floors above me. If you're really observant, you'll see we share the same last name. We aren't related. We do use this coincidence to our advantage. On occasion, if it gets us out of a jam, we'll tell people we're brothers even though we look nothing alike. He is tall, skinny, has blond hair, and blue eyes. I'm short, have (had) brown hair, and brown eyes. He's a year younger than me. I have known him since I was five. Even though I'm a year older, he's considered the smart one. At least that's a role he's assumed and tries to keep current on.

That part started when I was six and in first grade. Our mothers would walk us home from school every day. Together, we would trek the two miles of city blocks, always looking for entertainment to keep us occupied. One day, I was quizzing him on spelling words I had learned. It didn't matter that he was in kindergarten and didn't have a chance. That wasn't the point. The point was to bust him and bust him good. Mission accomplished. He didn't know any of it and I won that round. At least that day, I did. My six-year-old self didn't know it but I had started an academic rivalry that would go on for decades to come. In fact, I'm convinced that any trivial argument we have today is rooted in that one event.

That night, he studied a spelling list of his own. He chose a list of words that would make a spelling-bee champ nervous. The next day, I didn't waste any time breaking out the new words for the day on my friend (victim). I thought it would be 'easy pickings' yet again. Good for a least ten blocks of entertainment for the long hike home. It turned out to be a walk I'd never forget. As soon as I asked the first word, which by luck he got, he had a word of his own to ask me.

"Can you spell encyclopedia?"

Encyclo-what? How the hell does he know that? He doesn't know that. I figured I'd give it a go and if it was wrong, he'd wouldn't know it either. I'd be on to my next word for him, and the fun would continue. After I spelled it wrong, he corrected me, and spelled it right!

Of course, my ego didn't believe it. I had to have it verified by his mom. He had a couple more for me that I also got wrong. I don't remember those. But encyclopedia has been etched into my mind ever since, like a trigger word from a previous traumatic event. Needless to say, that put an end to my academic trivia for quite some time. To make matters worse, he used that same word on me, at random times over the next several years. I still managed to get it wrong every time.

Another topic that occupied us on those long walks home involved hypothetical animal 'cage fighting.' In our scenario, I estimated my family's toy poodle would, without a doubt, emerge victorious against his family's cat. We'd spend hours arguing about whose beloved family pet would win this epic canine v. feline deathmatch. Despite Jason being a cat person, if there was one type of pet that we could both agree on, it was tropical fish.

The tropical fish store in our neighborhood—Fish Town, USA—was only four blocks from our apartment building. As we got older and got cut loose to wander the neighborhood, it became a regular hang out for us. We'd always end up there to look at the fish, especially during the summer when we were bored. One summer, when I was thirteen and he was twelve, we finally decided to both take the plunge. We made multiple trips to Fish Town looking at our respective gravel colors, bowls, and fish colors. After a week of intense deliberation, we finally made the big purchase and both got Siamese fighting fish.

Two weeks into fish ownership, I was cleaning Clyde's bowl. In the process, I dropped it, and it shattered. Don't worry, Clyde, at this point, was resting comfortably in a paper Dixie cup. I did what any person and true fish enthusiast would do in this situation, I called Jason. I told him I had just broken my fishbowl, and I needed a new one, STAT!

Whether or not I told him that Clyde was in a paper cup has been a point of contention for the last thirty years. Jason, picturing my beloved new fish flopping on the floor gasping for air, knew at this point he was Clyde's only hope to avoid the dreaded toilet-bowl funeral.

He heroically hung up the phone, took the elevator downstairs, ran four blocks to Fish Town, purchased a new bowl (and gravel, just in case), ran four blocks back, took the elevator up to my floor, ran to my apartment, and then rang the bell. Bringing us to my argument in this legendary tale: how he thought a fish could possibly survive outside of water for his fifteen-minute roundtrip.

As Jason was gasping for breath, I answered the door. "Thanks, man! Why do you look like you're about to die, bro?"

"Because… [pant, pant,] I just ran [pant]… to the freaking fish store and …back! Is he OK? Quick! [pant] Put him the bowl!" he said, handing me the glass bowl and paper bag of gravel. He was confused when I tried to explain that Clyde was, in fact, fine and was never flopping on the floor as he had pictured it.

31

There are no words to describe the look of disappointment, horror, and anger on twelve-year-old Jason's face when he walked into my room and Clyde looked at him from inside that Dixie cup. I'd like to tell you thirty years later he's got over that. He hasn't. I still hear about it, regularly.

Summer of 1988, Midtown Manhattan

I was fifteen, and Jason was fourteen. Like every summer, we were wandering the streets of New York City. We were on the way back from some non-descript activity that had got us both out of our apartments. On the way home, we'd always go through a driveway that cut the block across our street in half. As we were walking through the driveway, a familiar Dominican voice yelled at us. "Hey! Youse guys. Look! Look!"

It was the doorman from the building associated with the driveway. We had a love-hate relationship with this particular doorman. It was the classic frenemy-type situation for us. Half the time he was friendly and the other half he'd spend hassling us for something we were doing around his building, that he didn't necessarily agree with. Whether it was riding a skateboard, a water-gun fight, a snowball fight, or just loitering, we'd hear about it from Joe. Especially if one of the tenants 'accidentally' got hit by water or a snowball.

At first, I thought he had an issue with something we had done earlier in the week. Most likely, one of the tenants had ratted us out, yet again. I thought back and couldn't think of anything we'd done. At least not anything recent. It didn't really matter what was going on. We looked at each other thinking, we'd better just run rather than deal with the impending beef awaiting us. Just as we were about to bolt, curiosity got the better of us. We both turned around, to see Joe walking toward us and pointing across the driveway at something. Joe was, best guess, in his thirties at the time. He was well over six feet tall. His height as well as his official doorman uniform, complete with tie and jacket, made him seem intimidating. But to us, he was just "Joe" and we knew there was little he could actually do to us.

"Look, man! Right there. You see that?!" I immediately thought we should have run when we had the chance. He was going to pin something on us that we didn't do. He was pointing at a waist-high concrete ledge and planter on the other side of the driveway. Trying to stay one step ahead of him, I started looking for graffiti. Thinking we'd be falsely accused of tagging up the neighborhood, yet again.

He continued in his thick Dominican accent, now standing next to us. "You guys blind, or what? Look, man, it's a pigeon. He's hurt, man. He can't fly. Maybe…maybe you kids do something eh? To help this guy out."

"What? I don't know about all that, man. What are *we* going to do?" I looked at Jason, who as always was the silent one, especially in these situations. I knew I was going to have to do all the talking to get out of this responsibility. Don't get me wrong, I was always an animal lover and even back then I wanted to be a vet. I even had a bird of my own at the time, a lovebird named Spanky. But this was different, right? This was a New York City street pigeon.

Most New Yorkers consider pigeons to be 'rats with wings.' All our lives we were instructed by our parents that pigeons were nasty and carried diseases. Basically, keep your distance and mind your own business. Which, actually, is the basic code of being a New Yorker, and it applies to most everything in New York, including this particular situation.

I looked over at the pigeon who was edging further back toward the plants and trees in the planter. It was trying to seek shelter from us. It would flap its wings in a poor attempt to fly but it just ended up hopping further along.

I continued, "What are we going to do with it? We don't even know what's wrong with him. How are we going to fix that? Even if we knew what we were doing, we can't just keep it in our apartment. Can't you call someone?"

I thought those were all valid points of reason. Even Jason was nodding his head in agreement. He let out an "Exactly" at the end as if he was saying amen to a sermon. I thought that shifting the responsibility to the adult here would get us out of the situation we were unwillingly being dragged into. I thought to myself, again, we should have run.

"Who am I going to call?! No one going to care about some pigeon. Use your head, man. You kids can come up with somethin' to help this guy. Look at 'im. We got to help 'im."

Just then a UPS driver called Joe back to the building. He left us there, dumping the responsibility on us. Now we were trapped there with this pigeon. Jason looked at me, waiting for some stroke of genius.

"You're the animal lover. You got a bird. What should we do here?"

I paused and didn't answer right away. I was staring at the pigeon noticing his unique coloring. Where the majority of the city pigeons' heads and necks are a dark gray, this pigeon's head and neck were brown. His wings were also light brown, instead of the typical gray. Jason, trying to get me to answer looked down at his watch and said, "I gotta go, man. I guess I'll just leave you to it."

"How am I supposed to know? I have a lovebird, not a pigeon. This is way different. Can't sneak this into my house, it's a pigeon! What are we supposed to do? Don't these things carry diseases?" I may be the animal lover but he's the smart one here. Surely, he'd know if all that was just an old wives' tale.

"I'm thinking that's pretty much true. At least that's what my dad has always told me." His dad, like mine, was also a New Yorker from Brooklyn. Jason most likely got the same lecture on these pigeons as me. We sat there continuing to stare at this pigeon who was now nestled in the shrubbery of this planter, looking helpless. Slowly he started to evolve from a nasty flying rat, into a sick defenseless animal in need of help. I wanted to help but I didn't have the logistics mapped out to make it happen.

"Hey! You guys still there, huh? I thought you'd leave. Good!" Joe shouted as he reappeared from the building. This time he was carrying an empty box. "Here, man, we could use this." He started to move toward the pigeon and tried to herd him using the box.

"Use it for what?" I asked still trying to get a grasp on the situation.

"To catch him, man!"

"Then what? Where are *you* going to take him?"

"You kids are smart. You'll figure somethin' out. Help me get this bird, man! He may be sick but he's fast!"

Against our better principles of 'keeping our distance and minding our business,' we felt obligated to jump in to help him. The three of us scrambled after the pigeon as it hopped and flew like a chicken down the driveway. Fortunately, before it made it down the driveway, and out into traffic, it stopped. It sat at the end of the driveway, panting and hopeless.

Joe handed me the box. I was reluctant to do anything with this bird, never mind put it in a box. Joe sensing my fearful pause hit me on the arm and said, "Get on with it, man! Before he gets away again!" I reluctantly scooped him into the box using the flap.

"There you go, bro. Nice! I knew you guys could handle it," he triumphantly stated. Just then, one of the tenants in the building called for Joe. It was perfect timing for him to bail. He turned to us and said, "You guys got it from here, right? Good, good!" It was a rhetorical question because he didn't really give us an opportunity to decline. We blindly nodded our heads in agreement, and just like that we'd assumed full responsibility for the 'case.'

"What are we going to do? You got a plan for this?" I asked Jason, holding the box and nudging him with it. I was hoping for some idea, anything. He must have something since he agreed.

"I got nothing for you, man. You were nodding *your* head so I just went along with it," he replied, shrugging his shoulders.

We walked to the other end of the driveway and sat down on the planter with the box beside us. As we sat trying to decide what to do next, periodically, we'd hear the pigeon shuffling in the box.

We immediately figured out how we'd care for him. That was the easy part. I had birdseed at home from my bird. We also planned on lining the box with newspaper to catch all the droppings. The real issue we were having was where we'd keep or, rather, hide him.

We knew our neighborhood inside and out. Even though we were in New York City, you'd be amazed at the small spaces, little parks, and courtyards scattered about the city. You could have something in plain sight and the majority of people wouldn't even know it was there. The problem was we needed a place that *guaranteed* it wouldn't be found, and that seemed impossible. Any idea we came up with was immediately shot down by the probability of some janitor, construction worker, lunch breaker, smoker, or random homeless person finding our patient.

Finally, it hit me. "I got the perfect place! How could we have been so stupid? Right behind our building. In the courtyard," I said, pointing across the street.

"You mean behind the garage?" Jason took a pause, and when he answered, "That could actually work," I thought I had made the perfect choice. We found out later that this location wasn't as perfect as we had thought it would be.

Next door to our building was a public garage. It had a small driveway that was nestled between our building and the one next door. People paid either by the hour or long-term by the month, to park their cars there. It consisted of a small lot behind our building, and an elevator that led to more parking spaces underground. Behind our building, and behind this garage, was a twenty-foot-square courtyard.

Only the garage attendants went back to the garage to get the cars and bring them out onto the street. The courtyard was elevated, and the property belonged to our building. The attendants never hung out there. They had a makeshift office shack that was on the driveway. They spent most of their free time in there.

"What about Pugsley?" Jason asked trying to sure up our choice and cover all possibilities.

'Pugsley' as we'd nicknamed him, was one of the maintenance men who worked in our building. He was short, balding, rarely shaved, and had a pot belly of gigantic proportions. He was from somewhere in eastern Europe, and his thick accent made it hard to understand what he was actually saying. We referred to him as Pugsley because of his stature. The name came from the beloved character on the TV show, *The Addams Family*.

We didn't have nicknames for everyone in our neighborhood, albeit potentially negative ones like in the case of Pugsley. But, like Joe across the street, we had a rocky relationship with Pugsley. He was pleasant enough if you were on his good side. Even though we had no idea what he was saying most, if not all, of the time, he would always end it with a hearty laugh. He wasn't always laughing, though, and if we ever did anything he didn't necessarily agree with he'd be the first one to rat us out.

The perfect example of this occurred one summer when we were a lot younger. We had come up with a game (a form of entertainment) that involved dangling action figures and various other toys eleven stories down from my bedroom window into the courtyard. Aside from the obvious, the other bad idea was using my mother's sewing thread that wasn't strong enough to support the weight of the toys. By the end of this game, my entire toy collection ended up lying in the courtyard.

Jason heroically volunteered to go downstairs and collect them. He was busted by none other than Pugsley. In a stroke of genius (told you he was smart), Jason tried to explain that we were babysitting for a young child in the building who had thrown my toys out the window. He assured Pugsley that we had it all under control. We had already reprimanded this kid and it would never happen again.

I don't know if it was the language barrier, or Pugsley was smart enough to know we weren't old enough to babysit anyone, but he didn't buy Jason's explanation. We weren't supposed to be in that courtyard, never mind throwing toys out the window onto it. He responded by yelling at Jason in his native tongue and then throwing in some choice American curse words for good measure. Jason hopelessly collected the toys into the garbage bag I'd provided him and left.

Pugsley, as expected, ratted us out. He didn't waste any time either. Since it was my apartment, he anxiously waited in the lobby for my father to return home from work. Subsequently, my dad gave me a lecture about dangling toys out the window. He ended it by asking me if he was raising some dumb moron who wanted to fall out the window dangling toys like a schmuck!? Needless to say, it wasn't a fun lecture or punishment, and I knew who to thank, Pugsley!

After all these years, we knew Pugsley's routine around the building. Realistically, he had no real business (job responsibilities) in that courtyard. In that little toy situation, getting caught had more to do with a tenant complaining about seeing a GI Joe dangling outside their window, than Pugsley's great detective work.

We officially decided that the garage was as close to a guarantee as we would get. We were right, Pugsley never found out. It was someone else, who we never suspected would care. They would end up making things more difficult by meddling with our case and potentially changing its outcome.

I grabbed the box and we strolled across the street. We walked down the driveway and walked past the little shack. We could hear salsa music blasting from it as we snuck past. It was summer and the garage attendants were huddled up in the shack trying to milk what cold air they could out of the jacked-up air conditioning they had. We got to the courtyard and Jason was going to wait with the box while I went upstairs to get the supplies for our patient.

"Don't worry, I'm sure I'll be perfectly fine. I'll just wait here for Pugsley. Hopefully, that conversation goes better than the last time," he said to me sarcastically as I left.

I returned, juggling the margarine containers of birdseed and water. I was also carrying four pages from the *New York Post,* and my mother's stolen kitchen gloves. I didn't know if pigeons really did carry any diseases but I wasn't about to take any chances.

Upon my return, Jason greeted me with, "Dude, I got some good news and some bad news." I immediately started to think that someone had already busted us.

"I've been here looking up and remembering that fun time *you* had with the toys and I had an awesome idea. We should run a string from your room down to the box. Then, you can pull the string up, open the lid, and check on him. Make sure he's OK, and if he's still here. All right from the convenience of your room. How do you like that?!" he said, punching my shoulder for effect.

"That is an awesome idea. I like it! So, what's the bad news?"

"See ya!" he replied giving me a wave goodbye. "You're going to have to go all the way back upstairs and drop that string down to me. Then, we are going to need some tape. Have fun, bro."

It was an ingenious idea. I was relieved that was the only bad news. I didn't even mind going back upstairs in the elevator again. I made it back up to my apartment. I got the old brown package string from my dad's tool drawer. He wouldn't miss it. In the old days, my parents used the string to tie around packages like a handle. I don't know when that all went out of style but I did know he wouldn't miss the string.

I opened the window to my bedroom. For a joke, I tied an old GI Joe figure and threw him down to Jason. The other end was attached to the roll that I placed on the floor. He caught the GI Joe and gave me the thumbs up.

I went back downstairs to the courtyard with tape. We gently dumped the pigeon out of the box. By some miracle, the box was still clean and free of any droppings. I lined the bottom with the newspaper. I was wearing the big, yellow kitchen gloves, and was braver this time getting him in. It was difficult at first. He had regained some strength and started bolting from us like a chicken. He came close to leaping from the courtyard into the garage but I caught him in the box. I set him up with the containers of seed and water. We partially closed the lids of the box and attached the string. After the string was pulled, the weight of the lid would allow it to close on its own.

By now it was late afternoon, and we decided we better leave before the garage started to get busy from rush hour. We didn't want to risk getting spotted by an attendant and draw attention to our patient. We had done all we could for him. As with many cases, it was now up to him. In our particular situation, without any veterinary knowledge, we also had to depend on luck.

That evening, I was constantly leaning out the window to check on him. I had the room all to myself that summer. My older brother was on a college internship in Washington DC. My brother wouldn't have done anything to interfere but it's always less of a hassle when you don't have a roommate to explain things to. Especially if that roommate likes to give you a hard time like an older brother. My dad was a different story.

As soon as he came home, he caught me hanging out the window. He must have immediately thought I was nostalgic for my younger days and was hanging stuff out the window again.

"Hey, schmuck! What the hell are you doing now?!" he yelled in his unmistakable, thick Brooklyn accent. My father may have only been five-foot-three but he was intimidating. I turned around instantly. I immediately tried to explain everything.

He didn't believe any of it and thought I was trying to fabricate an elaborate cover story. When I showed him the pigeon in the box down in the courtyard below, he was amazed. He was immediately impressed with the idea of string attached to box. When he pulled on it to test it himself, he smiled. His attitude changed once he realized that an actual live pigeon was on the other side.

"You realize those things carry diseases, right, genius?"

In case you were wondering about that, according to the New York City Department of Health, pigeons do in fact carry diseases. Histoplasmosis, cryptococcus, and psittacosis are the big three. Catching any one of those is rare unless you are immunocompromized. Psittacosis would carry the highest risk of those three. In New York City, psittacosis is quite rare with, on average, approximately one human case identified each year. Routine cleaning of droppings doesn't pose a serious health risk to most people. For the record, the Centers for Disease Control and Prevention (CDC) advise simple precautions with cleaning droppings, such as wearing disposable gloves and "washable clothes." One last point, in case you were also wondering, in New York City it is not illegal to feed or keep pigeons.

Of course, my father didn't know any of those specific details at the time. He knew that they carried *something* and wanted to make sure I kept my distance from whatever that something was. At first, he tried to convince me that we'd done enough already. Like in similar situations of potential emotional attachment he broke it to me 'gently.'

"Look, Peter, I know you want to help this thing out. But, it's either going to make it or…it's not going to be so lucky. He's probably going to croak. You gave him a shot with the food and water and all that. Maybe, maybe just see what happens."

I didn't go through all this to see 'what happens.' This was my case now and I was going to see it through. After a lengthy discussion, he

41

finally relented, most likely thinking there was a good chance he'd 'croak' by morning.

"That's no pet bird. Don't go touching it or anything. Especially if it croaks! Oh, by the way, when your mother finds out you took her gloves she's going to be pissed," he said as he left my room smiling. At that point I knew, as always, I had his full support.

The next morning, I woke up and immediately went to the window to check on him. I lifted the lid and continued to stare down at the box to confirm he moved.

I immediately picked up the phone and called Jason. "He made it, bro! He made it. He's still alive!"

"Nice. Why wouldn't he make it? I didn't think he'd actually die overnight. Did you?"

My dad's discussion had impacted me more than I realized. I quickly changed the subject and we agreed to meet downstairs in twenty minutes. After we met up, we began a routine we'd repeat three times a day, over the next several days. We would alternate by either taking the service door in our building or sneaking down the driveway. The route depended on our visual recon, whether it was Pugsley or the attendants who we needed to avoid.

After that, the routine was exactly the same. Detach string. Don big, yellow kitchen gloves. Remove birdseed and water. Remove pigeon. Change out *NY Post*. Replace pigeon. Replace new seed and water. Remove gloves. Reattach string. Sneak past shack. Depose of garbage bag in New York City garbage receptacle on the street corner.

As the animal lover and aspiring veterinarian in this operation, I was arbitrarily assigned to all these tasks. Jason provided moral support, served as a lookout, and helped chase the pigeon when needed. That first morning, Jason reminded me of something we had neglected to handle the very first day. As the die-hard animal lover, I couldn't believe I had overlooked this one, but he was right.

42

"What are we naming him? I mean this guy needs a name, right?" he asked me as I was replacing the birdseed. We didn't know— actually know—if it was a male or female but we'd arbitrarily and subconsciously assigned his gender as male from the beginning.

We went through a laundry list of names until finally, Jason suggested the eventual winner. "I got it, Dude! That's it! Dude, that's perfect."

"What's perfect?! What's the freaking name?" I asked, laying the gloves behind the box.

A brief comedy routine ensued, as it took me a few go-arounds to process that 'Dude' was the actual name he was suggesting, rather than him using the popular eighties salutation for your homeboy. Since we were in the middle of the decade of 'awesome,' 'radical,' and 'dude,' it was a great suggestion. I quickly embraced the choice and, from that moment on, the legend of Dude officially began.

The case was going quite smoothly. By the second day, in my UN-professional opinion, Dude appeared to be improving. It became harder to catch him. His attempts to escape resembled more of a flying bird than a chicken scrambling away. In the afternoon that day, we decided to rip one of the lids off the top. In this way, only half the box was covered. We figured he could shelter on one side and could easily leave out of the other side if he wanted.

That afternoon, I continuously checked on Dude from my bedroom window. Each time, I expected to see an empty box but I didn't. That evening when we went downstairs, I was even wondering if we'd find him gone. We had a surprise that evening, alright, and it wasn't a good one.

I had just started the routine of taking care of Dude and talking with Jason. I went through the motions of what had already become second nature. Out of nowhere, and without warning, we heard, "Cho, Man! We like that. We like your little bird, man!" one of the garage attendants called out, Hispanic accent obvious. He walked up the ledge and continued to stare at us without saying a word. It was obvious he was trying to intimidate us and give us a hard time. He was off to a good start.

"Ah, shit! Great," Jason murmured to me, as he anxiously signaled for me to hurry up. I had just dumped Dude from the box. Dude had found the fresh seed behind me and was inquisitively pecking at it.

"Yeah, man, we've been checking him out. Man, he looks pretty good," he continued.

Another shorter and fatter attendant arrived and decided to join in on the fun. "Yeah, bro, he's lookin' good. Nice and fat. Just how we like to…eat them! You know we eat those birds in Puerto Rico," he declared proudly as if it was a well-known fact.

As a wise-ass teenage New Yorker, I normally would have enjoyed this opportunity to engage in 'friendly banter' with these two individuals. However, I had no idea how far they'd go to mess with us when we were gone. I was fairly certain they weren't going to eat him. But I didn't know if they'd hide or dump him somewhere out of spite. I chose to ignore them and hoped they'd go away but they didn't.

I had just arrived at the part of the routine where I'd catch Dude with the box. Of all the times, we went to catch him, that one by far was the most difficult. In an effort to speed things along, Jason wasted no time rushing in to help.

"Ha, ha! Yeah, man! Chase that sucker! That will help build up his legs. Perfect!" the taller and skinnier attendant called out as they both continued to laugh, enjoying the show.

I was hoping Dude would fly away and put an end to all of this but he didn't. The show continued. For the next few minutes, they continued to run their colorful commentary. To us, it seemed like an eternity. After we got him in the box, we hastily finished up and left the courtyard.

As we left, they lagged along behind us, as if they were personally escorting us down the driveway. Their commentary continued.

"Thanks for fattening him up for us. You don't have to come back tomorrow. Unless you want us to... to save you some of our lunch!" the tall one exclaimed.

Uncharacteristically, Jason turned and yelled, "We'll see about that! Anything happens to that bird, I'll make sure...make sure, your ass gets fired!"

They all paused for a second. Like me, they were both caught off guard by Jason's response. They had a blank look on their faces, and for that brief second, they just stared at each other. Then they both immediately burst out laughing. The fatter one started saying something to us in Spanish before they both started laughing again. Dejected, we both walked away. We could still hear them laughing as we walked into our building.

The next morning, when I looked out the window, Dude was still in the box. I met Jason downstairs and, as luck would have it, Pugsley was hovering around the service door. This meant we would have to go down the driveway. We knew we were on their radar now. We tried to sneak past the shack but it was pointless. We had become a new form of amusement for them. As soon as we made it past the shack, the door swung open behind us and we heard the music inside go from 'really loud' to 'even louder.'

"Cho, man! We told you not to come back!" the tall attendant yelled out to us as we went into the courtyard.

"I thought you told us you were going to eat him?" I replied gently dumping Dude from the box.

"Yeah, what's up with that?" Jason chimed in.

"We were but my man is off today so, that's all happening tomorrow, bro! I got *this* guy with me today and he don't eat no pigeons. All he eats is McDonald's," he said, laughing at his own joke as he pointed to the new, third attendant.

45

"Yeah, I don't eat those," attendant number three answered flatly in his thick Latin accent. It was clear that the new guy wasn't as willing a participant as that short fat guy from the day before. He was older than the other two. His obvious middle age and thick mustache, it seemed, made him too sophisticated to play along. They continued to watch us tend to our daily routine with Dude in silence.

The new guy grew bored rather quickly. He left and went back to the shack, leaving only the tall one to harass us. He quipped at us a few times but realizing he had no audience to egg him on, he left too. As he walked away he turned and boldly announced, "Say goodbye to your little friend, man. Tomorrow is his big day!" To make his point, he drew a line across his neck with his index finger.

For the next twenty-four hours, all I could think about was if that guy was really demented enough to take Dude. I was still, fairly, certain he wasn't going to eat him. I was still concerned they'd get rid of him one way or another out of spite. Jason also had his reservations but he wasn't as worried, "They aren't going to do anything, man. They are just messing with us. Trust me. They aren't going to touch that pigeon. They're all talk, man. I'll talk to you tomorrow. Later." That was how Jason ended our phone call that night. I'm sure he slept better than I did.

I woke up early but, even at six-thirty, I was worried it wasn't early enough. I went right to the window. I could already see cars driving down the driveway and the attendants scrambling around. I opened the window and frantically pulled up on the string. The flap opened and Dude was gone!

I immediately called Jason. He didn't believe me at first. Even when we met downstairs, I got the impression that, in his mind, he was playing along with a joke. He was waiting to get to the courtyard, to see Dude, and hear me say, "Psych! I got you."

After we went through the service door, I ran up to the box and pulled the flap back to show him. He looked at the empty box, and flatly stated, "Man, I thought you were messing with me. He is gone…really gone. I guess…I guess he made it." We stood silently staring at the empty box.

We both had the same mixed emotions. We wanted to be happy but we both didn't definitively know whether he had flown away or if something else had happened. Just then the tall and short attendants walked up to the edge of the courtyard.

"I told you we were going to eat your friend, man. He was good!" the tall one exclaimed.

"Yeah, we couldn't wait for lunch so, we had him for breakfast. Best breakfast ever!" the short sidekick explained, as he rubbed his fat stomach, and they both started laughing.

"What did you really do with him?!" I asked frustrated, worried that they had him stashed somewhere. They both continued to laugh.

"Seriously, man, where is he? I'm not playing. Where'd you put him?"

They started talking to each other in Spanish and started laughing again. Just then another attendant called out, "Que pasa!? Vamonos!" He threw the tall one a set of keys and the short one scrambled to a car that had just pulled into the driveway.

"They're full of shit. They didn't do anything to him, man. Trust me. Those guys would be too scared to even touch a pigeon, never mind catch him. He made it. I know he did. Let's go." At that point, I didn't know if Jason was trying to convince me or himself.

"You're probably right. I guess he made it," I replied, still not completely convinced of the outcome.

I gathered up Dude's box and tossed the kitchen gloves in. As we walked down the driveway with the box, I thought that would be the time one of the attendants might confess and end their long-running joke. That never happened. They ignored us and continued retrieving and parking cars as if we weren't even there. We walked down to the street corner. I unceremoniously threw the box and all of Dude's accessories into the trash can. Just like that, my first 'case' had officially concluded.

We still, to this day, believe he flew away on his own accord. For what it's worth, Joe also believed he made it. When we told him the story, he was certain about it. He had explained to us, in (way too much) detail, that one of his former girlfriends was in fact, from Puerto Rico, therefore, making him an absolute authority on all things Puerto Rican. He concluded by definitively stating, "I know those garage guys over there. They're all full of shit! They don't eat no pigeons in Puerto Rico. They didn't do anything to him, man. They are trying to mess with you guys, man. You know that. That guy made it! You guys did it!"

Subsequently, Joe treated us like rock stars for a few weeks after that. I'd like to say that Dude gave us a free pass with Joe in that driveway for life. It didn't. A couple of months later, Joe was back to busting on us now and again as he saw fit.

In captivity, pigeons commonly live up to fifteen years. On the streets, (urban population) pigeons rarely live more than four years. Thirty years later, Dude is no longer with us. However, it doesn't stop me. Whenever I spot a brown pigeon in New York City, I'll still habitually point and hit Jason in the arm and exclaim, "Look, man! It's Dude!"

Jason, in the courtyard, exactly thirty years later. The garage guys were a no-show for the thirty-year reunion. Pugsley not only declined our invitation but he refused to clean up the place!

WWGD (What Would Grandpa Do?)

I don't know how it will be for the next veterinary generation but it seems my generation got the short end of this stick. We are caught between two very different medical philosophies: the good ol' days where a magic pill or shot could treat just about everything, and the fancy modern times where we focus on getting an actual diagnosis. However, in an effort to achieve that goal, things can get complicated, and that may mean spending more money. Unfortunately, for some owners it's hard to see the benefit of paying all that extra money, especially, when grandpa could have done, what they perceive as the same thing, for a lot less. Besides, it's never that complicated when that old reality TV vet does it. So, that leaves me holding the bag, trying to explain what modern veterinary medicine has to offer to these holdouts from the good old days. Which is exactly what happened with Mr. Simmons.

That Little Summer Two Years Ago

As fate would have it, one old veterinarian in my 'area' was retiring. By area, I mean within a forty-minute drive from my practice. Despite numerous veterinarians being in closer proximity to him, this vet arbitrarily recommended me to all his clients. Because of the distance, we only had thirty phone calls from his clients. Approximately fifteen made actual appointments. Unfortunately, only a few made the cut to become long-term clients.

The rest were unimpressed with the advantages that modern medicine had to offer. They longed for the days in their last practice where things were less complicated, a lot cheaper, or, better yet, even free. Their old vet seemed to fix everything with one injection, and without doing any tests. They definitely weren't a fan of the "fancy vet" and "all them lengthy explanations."

They were all quite disappointed because their vet had told them all so much about me. Apparently, not only had he known me but had also gone to vet school with me. We were classmates, colleagues, and even close friends. He even claimed he took me fishing one time. "They would be in good hands with Dr. Miller. He's a great guy," he told them. I can't argue with that but I'd never met him. Furthermore, he was a typical Southerner and had graduated from Georgia. I graduated from vet school in Scotland. He was also a good twenty years older making being present in his graduating class impossible. It didn't matter. As far as these clients were concerned, if "good old doc" had said it, then it was true.

Liz had heard it all so many times, that she even started to believe it. The first few calls, she would correct them and would repeat my name over and over but it didn't matter. The response was the same: "Yes. I was referred to *Dr. Miller* by my previous vet. Dr. Miller is a friend of his, they went to vet school together at Georgia."

She started to believe I was holding back information from her. She concluded I was being lazy and didn't want to see more appointments. She continued to interrogate me, trying to piece together this mysterious puzzle. She'd constantly bombard me with the same line. "They all say he knows you. You *sure* you don't know him?" She hoped eventually I'd crack under her pressure and reveal how I was mysteriously connected to this vet.

Wednesday 8:32 am

Upon arrival, I went straight to the computer in the treatment area to check the appointments. The first appointment read: *"Emergency Exam. New Client. Referred by Dr. Hill. Hit by car in driveway approx. 10 pm last night. Seems painful on the right side. Not eating. Lethargic."*

Jen was loitering by the exam-room door. She pulled the chart from its holder on the door and waved it at me to get my attention. "I don't know why you need to read it on the computer every time. It's all *right* here. Don't worry, we checked him in, and he's stable. His gums look OK to me. He's standing in there just wagging his tail. Thank God, it's not a *real* emergency. We'd be in trouble with the way you roll in here."

I took the chart from Jen. It matched what was written on the computer. Jen had added that his gums were pink, along with his weight, and a normal temperature. We went in, and just as Jen had described, Murphy was standing there wagging his tail. Murphy was a big eleven-year-old black lab. Even if I didn't already know his age, I could tell he was older by the gray on his muzzle and around his eyes. He inquisitively walked over to me and licked the back of my hand as I stroked his head.

"Nice to finally meet you, Dr. Miller. Dr. Hill has told me all about you! He said you're a great guy and I'd be in good hands," Mr. Simmons stated, as he extended his hand for a handshake. His accent was bland and lacked the southern twang of the true locals in our area. My guess was he was transplanted from somewhere in the Midwest.

"I can't argue with that. That's all true," I jokingly replied. Jen smirked and then rolled her eyes in response. It was obvious she was no longer amused by the played-out line I had been using on all the recent referrals. Rather than correct these people, on the obvious misinformation their vet had given them, I just went along with it. There was no other vet their doctor had mistaken me with. I figured this old timer must have seen our practice online and decided we were the best bet for his clients. Why he fabricated the cover story is beyond me. I definitely wasn't going to start correcting these people now.

Ron Simmons slowly sat down on the exam-room bench. Like Murphy, he was also showing the signs of getting older. He looked to be in his early seventies. He was thin, and his short gray hair was parted to the side. He was wearing khaki camping shorts, a tucked in blue polo shirt, and thick black-rimmed Ray-Ban-style glasses.

I pulled out the copies of the records from Dr. Hill's practice. As I looked through the history, I asked, "Any past major medical problems or issues with Murphy I need to know about?" I asked knowing the old

53

grandpa vets are sometimes 'selective' on what they chose to put in their records.

"Nope. Just the arthritis in his hips. That's it. He's on anti-inflammatory medication. We did his blood work last year, around Christmas, and everything was normal."

"Can you describe what happened? Did you see when he was hit by the car?"

"Yeah. I mean, no… well, I was there but, I was…in the truck actually. I mean …it sounds kind of dumb…but I was backing out of the driveway. He's always right there, I should have known. But it was dark, and I couldn't see him. I heard him cry out as soon as it happened. I think…I might have hit him with the back bumper of my pick-up. I don't think I actually ran him over. I was only going maybe five miles an hour if that. He could have been under the tire but I don't know that I ran him over. Boy, that sounds bad, doesn't?"

"It happens. It's actually more common than you think. How did he do overnight?"

"Murphy seemed OK last night. I checked him in the middle of the night. Trust me, Doc, if he'd looked like he was in real distress, I would've taken him to those emergency vets. They're so darn expensive though, I figured we could ride it out until morning. This morning he had trouble standing up. He didn't touch his breakfast. He also cried out when I touched him on the right side, by his chest. So, I figured he was banged up a bit, maybe bruised. So, I called first thing."

I examined Murphy. I couldn't localize any areas of pain or discomfort. He seemed stiff in his hind legs, with a slight limp on his right hind leg. I couldn't definitively tell if that was from the accident or his ongoing arthritis. The other thing that concerned me was that his gums seemed slightly pale. In some pets, their gums can have a lot of black pigment instead of being all pink. This makes it difficult sometimes to accurately assess their gum color. Murphy was one of those.

"Mr. Simmons, he appears to be OK but I am concerned about his gums. More specifically, with internal injuries, he could be slowly bleeding internally. It wouldn't be obvious at first like with a major injury but it's possible. I'd like to look at his blood work and take some X-rays of his chest and abdomen."

"I don't know. You think all that is necessary? Maybe you just give him a shot for pain and we see how he does?"

"I do think it's necessary. The other benefit of the blood work is we can also check how his liver and kidneys are handling the arthritis medication. If that's all OK, it gives us the opportunity to increase his dose. Let me get you up a treatment plan so, you can see where we're at."

Jen instinctively took her cue and left to go print out a copy of the treatment plan. As I turned to leave behind her, Mr. Simmons stopped me at the door. "It's OK, Doc. I already decided. Do whatever it takes. You're probably right. We should check him out."

"That's fine. We'll get you a treatment plan anyway so you can see where you're at." I left the exam room and finished writing up the record.

A treatment plan is always a good idea in our practice especially with new clients whose previous vet may have had a completely different 'price structure.' By the way, 'treatment plan' is the politically correct term we use for an estimate.

This all started in our practice when Jen came across an article in one of the veterinary technician journals years ago. It discussed clients' supposed sensitivities and aversions to the nasty "E" word, 'Estimate.' It went on to describe the word as unprofessional and that it "should be deleted from your practice's vocabulary."

Jen is the last one to take advice from anyone, especially a journal. But, on occasion, if it's a really good suggestion, or at least if she thinks it is, she'll take it to heart. Needless to say, she has forced us all to use 'treatment plan' ever since.

I am all for political correctness, at least in my practice, but the problem is that most of the clients have no clue what a treatment plan is. Because of this, I'm in a never-ending losing battle between keeping Jen off my back and getting clients to understand what a treatment plan is. I will confess, whenever Jen isn't around, I still use the E word quite freely.

When Jen returned with the treatment plan, Mr. Simmons looked at it and signed off on it immediately. Jen came out walking Murphy on his leash. She led him to Cassey, who was already holding the syringe and tubes for his blood work. After which, they were off to radiology.

In between the beeping of the X-ray machine, I could hear Jen mumbling her standard laundry list of complaints from radiology. Her most common ones were in relation to how her age and seniority should preclude her from doing the monotonous duties in our practice, like taking X-rays. Another classic is when she disposes of women's equality in the workplace by stating, "If you were a true gentleman, and a good boss, you'd be doing the X-rays for me."

I had learned to tune all this out years ago. I had just started to drink the coffee I made and was in no position to change a system that worked perfectly fine without (for) me. Just then, Jen came out of radiology carrying the X-rays of Murphy's abdomen. She handed them to me.

"Sorry to interrupt your little coffee break, Dr. Miller. Here are your films. Let me know if they're OK."

I took the films to the viewer. Murphy's X-rays, for the most part, were normal. Miraculously, he had not suffered any fractures. There was one vague abnormality on the films that I knew was going to make the day a lot more complicated. I would find out later that it would become even more complicated than I had initially thought.

The details of the organs in his abdomen were hard to make out. The lack of clarity in his abdomen suggested that he might be bleeding internally. The change was mild but it was significant. I kept staring at the films, hoping to see things differently, almost wishing things would be normal. Jen interrupted me by handing me the next set of films, Murphy's chest.

"Let me know if those are all OK, 'cause we are not going to be standing around in these gowns waiting to hear we have to take them over. This thing is hot! I think you remember wearing this stuff, way back when," she said, referring to the lead safety gear, and taking a shot at my reluctance to help ease her workload. As I looked over the chest films, I gave her a thumb's up. She left yelling to Cassey, "We're good! You can take Murphy back to the exam room."

Murphy's chest was completely normal. As I left radiology, Cassey handed me Murphy's blood work. It had confirmed what I was seeing on the X-rays. It was also where things got complicated.

His red blood cell count was just below the low end of normal. The other problem was the level of his platelets. They were really low in number. Platelets are a blood component that stops bleeding by clumping and clotting blood-vessel injuries. Platelets are essential for preventing excess blood loss and repairing bodily damage. To some extent, a process of damage and repair is a constant ongoing process throughout the body. Without it, all those minute injuries would lead to devastating blood loss. Having too few platelets represents a condition called thrombocytopenia. A condition that, left untreated, can be fatal.

In Murphy's case, he had either bled into his abdomen or was still slowly bleeding into it. This would explain his low red blood cell count (RBC) and the fact that his platelets were low (used up). The other consideration would be an entirely different medical problem. He could have any number of diseases, causing thrombocytopenia.

Making the accident a coincidence and leading us to stumble upon something he already had.

I knew the next step would be to refer Murphy to our local veterinary specialist hospital. They could check his abdomen with an ultrasound and get more insight as to whether he was actively bleeding internally. Not to mention figure out if something more complicated was going on. It would also set Murphy up if he needed further care, such as a blood transfusion or surgery. Lastly, as a primary practice, we aren't staffed overnight to provide minute-to-minute care that Murphy might need.

In the good old days, Doctor Grandpa would have most likely sent this one home. He'd have given him some pills, belted out, "You watch where you back out from now on, Mr. Simmons, ya hear?" and then rolled on to the next appointment.

10:05 am

I took the lab work and X-rays into the exam room. Murphy greeted me again by licking my free hand. This time, it was as if there was food waiting for him wrapped inside the X-rays and lab work. I went over all the results with Mr. Simmons and showed him the X-rays. I went on to tell him that the next step would be a referral to the specialist. I already knew that part wasn't going to go over well.

As soon as I started to talk about the specialist, Mr. Simmons took off his glasses and rubbed the bridge of his nose. He squeezed his eyes shut and continued to rub the bridge of his nose with thumb and forefinger. He looked like he was trying to recover from a headache that I had just given him. What was only a matter of seconds seemed a lot longer, as I waited for his response. When he put his glasses back on and started talking, I was prepared for the worst.

"Look, Dr. Miller, I see where you're coming from. I get it. Don't get me wrong, I love my dog. He's like my family. In fact, he's really all I've got. Well, unless you count, Nicole, my girlfriend if you want to call her that. What I'm getting at, is if you think he *really* needs all

58

that…I'll do it, if I have to. But if we could do something simpler, I'd rather go that way. It's a lot of money for me…especially right now."

I was relieved I didn't get the other response I anticipated. My relief was replaced with a more familiar feeling of frustration. The frustration of finding the sweet spot between quality medicine, and owner economics. I had to devise a plan to satisfy both. This time I wasn't given the easy out, of a yes or no answer.

The specialist could be an option if he *really* needs it. This is where the doubt creeps in. Even I started to think, 'I'm reading too much into this case. Maybe I am that "fancy vet." A little too smart for my own good. His old vet would have sent this case home.' There is a good chance Murphy would have been fine on some pills and good advice.

"I hear where you are coming from. I understand completely. It's a reality of veterinary medicine. One we are accustomed to dealing with every day." As I responded, my mind was multitasking, devising a plan as I was relating to a situation I was all too familiar with.

"How about we hospitalize Murphy for the day here? We'll watch him closely. I'd like to also run a urine sample, just to be thorough, and look for any blood. I'll recheck his red cell count later this afternoon around two o'clock. If it drops, at that point I'd be pretty adamant about him going to the specialist."

"I like that idea, Doc. That sounds good. I don't want you to get the wrong idea. I love this dog. I do. If things change, and I really have to go take him … I'll find a way to make it happen."

"I completely understand. It's OK. I think we have a solid plan. He'll stay with us, and we'll talk at two."

With that, we admitted Murphy, and Mr. Simmons left. We started him on tramadol for pain and offered him a small amount of canned dog food. He inhaled the bland hospital diet, and he remained stable for the entire morning. I started thinking that maybe grandpa would have done well by sending this case home. I expected that afternoon his RBC was going to be the same. I was wrong.

1:30 pm

Jen, who really is an awesome technician, deep down inside, ran the blood work without me asking for it. I had just finished lunch in my office, and she had formally laid it out on the open record. When I entered the treatment area, I could see it waiting there for me. I knew the RBC was going to be lower.

Had it been normal, Jen would've put it in the inpatient rack. It would no longer be a priority waiting in medical limbo. She'd make a comment on it being normal like she *obviously* knew it would be. She'd then go on to harass me for discharge instructions for the patient who'd be going home later on. This wasn't one of those.

No, this time she stood silently waiting. Anytime Jen is quiet, it's never good news. Both his red blood cells and his platelets had dipped. It suggested, whatever was going on with Murphy was still happening. Jen watched me intently as I picked up the phone to call Mr. Simmons. She knew the next step would be to refer Murphy to a specialist but she was anxious to see if Mr. Simmons would actually take him. She wasn't the only one.

"Mr. Simmons, I just looked at Murphy's recheck blood work and I'm concerned that it's got a little lower. I expected it to be stable, or even slightly less, but this is significantly lower. Like we discussed this morning, the next step would be to take Murphy to the specialist."

I knew there would be a pause but this break in the conversation was awkward. I almost thought that his cell phone had dropped the call and used that as an excuse to restart the conversation.

"Yeah, I'm still here, Doc. Well…if you think all that is really necessary, I guess… I'll go. To be honest, Doc, I didn't think it'd go this far. I mean, he looked pretty good this morning. Well, go ahead and set it up, or whatever," he begrudgingly replied. It was obvious that he was reluctant to go and was starting to lose faith in the medical game plan.

"We'll get all your records, lab work, and X-rays together. I'll go ahead and call down to the specialists."

"I got it. I'm on my way. I'll be there in forty minutes." With that, he hung up. Jen who was listening in to my conversation had already started to gather all the components of Murphy's medical file.

I made the call to the specialists. It was Dr. Carry, an internal-medicine specialist, who came to the phone. I had referred to her many times before. I had never met her face to face but she always seemed upbeat and pleasant on the phone. I relayed what had gone on with Murphy in the last twenty-four hours. As I recited the history of 'backed over,' 'low red cell count,' and 'possible blood in abdomen,' she, as usual, was pleasant and accommodating.

I started to imagine what must be going through her mind hearing all that. "Another winner from Dr. Miller. What's this guy doing? This should have been referred hours ago. Better yet, this patient should have gone to the emergency clinic last night! Now he decides to refer this as an emergency this afternoon? Great!"

My thoughts were interrupted by Dr. Carry's reply.

"No problem, Dr. Miller. What time do you think they'll be here?"

I told her around three o'clock. Despite my best efforts, I had tried to set this case up and avoid a classic catastrophic veterinary impropriety; the dreaded late referral.

Referring a case, or better described as 'dumping a case' in the evening, is the worst thing you can do to a specialist. Sure, they understand if you get an emergency near closing and have to refer it, that's OK. But dumping a case near closing time, or on a Friday is not cool. The only worse impropriety would be dumping a case on a Friday holiday weekend. Some old grandpa veterinarians were notorious for sitting on cases, sometimes all week, only to dump them

61

on a Friday holiday weekend. With a three o'clock referral, I was skirting the line on dumping this case rather than referring it.

"No problem, Dr. Miller. Just send him straight over and let us know when he's on the way."

If she was indeed thinking what I suspected, she did a great job at hiding it. I got off the phone and did my two o'clock cat yearly appointment. It was thankfully straightforward and stress-free. I was expecting Mr. Simmons to be arriving any moment when I heard Liz call back on speakerphone. "Dr. Miller, It's Mr. Simmons. He's on line one. He wants to talk to you."

Up until then, I had been worried about not dumping this case on Dr. Carry. I didn't know that I was actually the one who was going to get dumped on.

2:10 pm

"It's Ron Simmons. I was calling about Murphy."

"He's doing OK. I spoke to Dr. Carry, the internal-medicine specialist. You're all set with Murphy," I replied, confused by why he was calling since he was set to arrive any minute. I was waiting to hear he'd had a late start or had been stuck in traffic. That wasn't even close to what I was about to hear.

"Doc, I have been doing a lot of thinking. To be honest, all this stuff is way over my head. It's kind of complicated for me… to understand exactly what is going on with Murphy and the whole specialist deal-lio. So, Nicole came over, and I have been talking it over with her. She was an army nurse, way back when, and she understands this stuff a whole lot better than I do. If you don't mind…I'd like you to go over it all with her…if that's OK... Nicole. Here. It's Dr. Miller."

Just like that, Nicole came crashing into the dynamic of this case.

"Hi, Dr. Miller. I'm an RN, so you can tell it to me straight!" she belted out in a thick southern accent. I recounted the entire case exactly as I had for Dr. Carry. I answered all her questions, many of which were above and beyond concerned-pet-owner questions. When someone claims medical cred. and their line of questioning approaches an interrogation, I confess, I will go into unnecessary detail and use extra medical terminology out of spite. This was definitely one of those. After her lengthy interrogation was over, Registered Nurse (RN) Nicole belted out her own treatment orders.

"That dog will be fine! He just needs some rest is all. So's that blood count of his can recover. I'll be staying here tonight. I can nurse him here. I can watch him as good as any of them veterinary nurses. I've seen a lot more than any of them have, that's for damn sure. I know what to look for if he goes downhill on us. If he does, we'll take him…take him to those emergency vets. Don't you worry. He'll be in good hands tonight, trust me. OK? Good. Here's Ron!" She handed the phone off before I could even respond. I had already got the impression that Nicole RN wasn't too interested in my medical input on this one.

"You good with that, Doc? I think that sounds reasonable to me," Mr. Simmons sheepishly asked, caught in the middle of two very different opinions.

"I don't think it's the best idea for Murphy. I really don't have a Plan B for you that I'm comfortable with. I'm worried he's bleeding internally…or potentially has something else more complicated going on. And we need to know. Unfortunately, if he ends up at the emergency clinic you may end up spending close to what you would at the specialist. The care at the emergency clinic is excellent, and they could give him a transfusion if he needs it…but, they don't have the internal-medicine doctors that the specialist hospital has. So, you may not get an answer as to what is going on with Murphy there, and still end up taking him to the specialist in the morning. I think in his case, it makes sense not only medically but also, taking everything into consideration, financially as well."

Economics is always a sensitive subject, especially with a new client but a reality that has to be addressed. For me, economics has always been like a member of the family that's a real jackass. No one ever wants them around but they're obligated to invite them because they're family.

"I'm sorry, Doc, I'm just not going to…not going to take him to the specialist today. If he ends up at the emergency clinic…then, we'll see. But for now, I'd just like to take him this evening and watch him here."

At this point, there was no use in trying to explain or convince him otherwise. Nicole RN had taken over the case and given him the plan that made the most sense to him. I suspected it may go this way from the start. What I hadn't expected was for him to consent to see the specialist and then change his mind at the last minute.

There are many phone calls I dread making and this one is definitely in the top five. Thankfully, it's pretty rare for a client to consent to go to a specialist and then bail at the last minute. I don't know how often this happens to the specialist but it's always an awkward and embarrassing call for me to have to explain how a client who was scheduled to go right then has now suddenly changed their mind.

When I called the specialists, I wanted to talk to Dr. Carry, and tell her all about Nicole RN. I was hoping maybe she'd understand, and even empathize with my situation. As I sat on hold, I realized all that extraneous info would only end up making the situation even more embarrassing. I decided to keep it simple. It was pointless either way because I ended up passing the info to a vet tech who took my call. Despite the fact my ego had checked out of this profession a long time ago, I still felt embarrassed after I got off the phone.

The new plan was to keep Murphy until we closed. We'd run his blood work one last time right before he left. If it had fallen more, drastically, Mr. Simmons would have to take him straight to the emergency clinic.

5:35 pm

Jen handed me the latest Complete Blood Count (CBC). Murphy's RBC had fallen a couple of more points. It was still considered a mild anemia, putting Murphy in the 'stable' category. His platelets, however, had also dropped a bit lower. Making thrombocytopenia a real possibility.

I set up a slide to look at his blood under the microscope. I was attempting to get a manual estimate of his platelets. In theory, you can count the number of platelets under a few microscope fields, and then use an equation to get an estimate on platelet numbers. For some vets, this can be quite useful. For me, it's more of a daunting task, whose results I never trust no matter how many times I do it.

I never had a lot of confidence, or skill, in getting CBC information from the microscope. I think this all stems from my traumatic experience in veterinary school. We were taught the tedious, manual way to obtain a CBC under the microscope.

"You never know when lab machines fail or are unavailable. You may need this in an emergency," we were told. Our professor also pointed out at the beginning of that lab class, that most of us would be able to do this quite easily, while others would probably never get the hang of it. He assured us not to worry, as those few who lacked this skill could still 'limp' their way through the world of private practice. My fate was sealed in that class when he checked my results and boldly stated, loud enough for everyone to hear, "Mr. Miller, make sure you do have good laboratory equipment behind you, *wherever* it is that you finally end up."

I was 'limping' through looking at Murphy's slide. I double checked the results and even had Jen check me. Both our results had it even slightly lower than the machine. The platelet count was pointing to thrombocytopenia. Just as I got done looking at Murphy's slide for the third time, Liz called back to tell me Mr. Simmons had arrived and was waiting for me in the exam room.

In the exam room, I went over the last CBC with Mr. Simmons. I went into the complicated explanation of low platelet numbers and thrombocytopenia. Mr. Simmons nodded his head throughout the explanation and he peppered in a few, "Yup, I gotcha," as if he was following along. But he wasn't really grasping anything I was explaining and was just trying to speed things along. When I finished, he had no questions about anything and stared at me with a blank look on his face.

I suggested we send Murphy's CBC to our outside lab and have their pathologist review his blood under the microscope. I started to explain that the pathologist can analyze the cell types and their specific changes under the microscope. This analysis may help us get an answer about Murphy. He cut me off before I finished.

"Yup, I gotcha. Do that."

Sensing I'd lost his attention long ago, I quickly went over the discharge instructions. He was going to continue Murphy on the Tramadol, and monitor him closely overnight for any change, especially his gum color. Any change at all, he was to take him straight to the emergency clinic. If he did well, I was going to recheck him first thing in the morning.

"Don't worry, Doc. Nicole is at the house. She's staying over, …Over *again*, tonight. We'll be, we'll be fine," he flatly stated, sounding more worried about spending another night with Nicole than Murphy ending up in the emergency clinic.

Just then, Cassey walked Murphy into the exam room. Murphy bolted straight to Mr. Simmons. He initially tried to jump up on him but the arthritis and events of the night before got the better of him. Instead, he bounced up and down on his front legs and intermittently nudged Mr. Simmons's hand with his muzzle.

"Thanks, Doc! I really appreciate it. You did a great job on this one. I can't thank you enough, for…for everything. We'll see ya around," Mr. Simmons stated as he walked out of the room. It was apparent that he felt Murphy would be OK and was already thanking me for a job well done. I wasn't as convinced.

Thursday 8:02 am

"Well, well, well… Look who came in early today. I'm actually impressed. It was a good try, Dr. Miller, but Murphy isn't here. I can't tell you what happened but I do know they didn't end up at the emergency clinic," Jen announced as I walked into the treatment area.

She was right. I came in early, worried Murphy had gone to the emergency clinic. They close an hour before we open, and I didn't want this case waiting around for my usual arrival time.

It had been a long night for me and I was anxious to get an answer on this case. I grabbed Murphy's chart and reviewed the CBC from the lab. It confirmed the last results we'd got on our machine but it had the platelets a couple of points higher than our machine, and several points higher than our estimate on the slide.

"At least we were close but looks like your professor was right, leave it to the pros," Jen commented as I looked over Murphy's result. She was making it obvious that she, as always, had already been the first one to read them.

I went on to read the pathologist's review.

> There is a regenerative anemia present. There is Thrombocytopenia. The cause is not apparent. Causes include increased consumption/destruction (immune-mediated disease, tick-related disease, neoplasia [cancer], infectious, trauma, drug toxicity). If persistent and unexplained, further diagnostics including a bone marrow aspirate should be considered. —Sarah Mathews DVM, Diplomat (Clinical) Pathology.

Translation: You're on the right track, Dr. Miller. That whole list of stuff you were thinking about yesterday, is the same list of stuff I got for you, and if this bleeding doesn't stop, this case really needs to go to the specialist. P.S. Grandpa might have been right—got lucky—sending this one home, 'cause if the bleeding stops, chances are he'll be fine.

8:30 am

Mr. Simmons showed up right on time for his appointment. I grabbed the record from Liz, who had just shown him into the exam room. I rushed straight in past her, without even acknowledging her. I was anxious to see how Murphy was doing, and after working with me for over eleven years, she was well-accustomed to my social improprieties.

Mr. Simmons was wearing the same khaki camping shorts but, this time, he had a dark-blue T-shirt with "Old dudes rule!" printed on the front. Murphy appeared a bit brighter that morning. He ran up to me and immediately started pushing my free hand with his muzzle.

"Good morning, Doc. Murphy did great. Ate his breakfast this morning like it was going out of style. Nicole left this morning, and we…we, my friend, are doin' great!"

I didn't know if he was alluding to her being gone for the day or gone for good. Either way, he was as happy about that as he was about Murphy's condition.

"We got back his blood work, it agreed with the results we got here. Unfortunately, we don't have any more clues to why his platelets are low. I'd like to recheck his CBC this morning and see where we're at."

He replied instantly, "Do what you gotta do, Doc."

Just as I went to take the leash, Jen came through the door. Fearing there might have been a lengthy discussion, she had opted to wait outside the exam room. She had been listening in outside the door and was waiting for her cue.

I handed her the leash and she went back to the treatment area to get his blood sample. After Jen and Cassey got his blood sample, I slipped in a recheck exam. It was completely normal. Even his gum color appeared normal. Murphy was taken back to wait with Mr. Simmons as I anxiously waited for the blood results. Hoping the results would put Murphy in the clear and rule out a more complicated diagnosis. I started to edge closer to the lab area, waiting for the machine to give the results I wanted.

"Dr. Miller! How many times do I have to tell you not to invade my personal space? You know I have a real issue with you hovering around me in MY lab area. You always insist on waiting right here in my lab area. It is not going to get you your results any faster. Right? Please, give me some space. I thought we had a deal about crossing the line? Remember? Here." Jen handed me the results, upset that I had broken our (her) agreement.

Murphy's red blood cells had improved, but only by a couple of points. His platelets had also only improved slightly. It wasn't enough. He was stable but still in the gray zone. It wasn't falling so I wouldn't be able to make a compelling argument to Mr. Simmons to take Murphy to the specialist, and it hadn't increased dramatically enough that I could make the argument to myself he'd be fine.

It was just as complicated as yesterday. I was prepared for that and had a game plan for Murphy if Mr. Simmons wasn't down with the specialist. But I wasn't prepared for when Mr. Simmons made things even more complicated. In fact, so complicated that he would leave us all in anguish for quite some time.

I went over the blood work, and despite my best efforts, it was obvious that in Mr. Simmons' mind, Murphy was just fine. It hadn't gone down, it was actually going up. Murphy, for all practical purposes, was a new dog. He didn't need to go the specialist. I had planned for that response.

"Mr. Simmons, that's OK. I understand. I would like to see Murphy back tomorrow morning then and recheck his blood work.

69

Then we can make a plan for the weekend." I figured I had one last chance to prove one way or the other what was going on. I could refer him Friday morning if I had to. It'd be another borderline dump but the morning is still acceptable as far as the specialist is concerned. His response was a clue that things were going to be even more convoluted.

"I can't come in tomorrow. I just can't."

There was a long pause. I immediately thought that as far as Mr. Simmons was concerned, he had gone far enough with us. Murphy was fine, and he would no longer be needing our services. Perhaps permanently. I was speechless for a second as his response had caught me off guard. Before I could try and reply, he started to smile and started back again.

"No, Doc, we just can't do that. I'm driving back to Ohio tomorrow, first thing in the morning. We have a family reunion of sorts…that I just can't miss. I haven't seen some of these people in years and I'm not getting any younger. I have to leave at five in the morning if I want to beat all the traffic. You know what it's like. You don't open till like eight so, that puts me way behind if I do that. It's just not possible."

I started to scramble for some sort of alternative plan. One that would satisfy the Simmons family reunion travel time and a medical plan. Mr. Simmons went on to discard the next viable plan, without me even suggesting it.

"I could have maybe, maybe even left Murphy with Nicole…but, after last night…that's out the window. I decided I'm taking Murphy with me. I don't think we'll be seeing her again, that's for sure. Right, Murphy?"

I was at a loss for words. I was legitimately worried that Murphy might be a ticking medical time bomb. When it went off, it would leave Mr. Simmons and Murphy in dire straits out on the road. I tried to use that fact as leverage for him to see the specialist. This way they'd get medical closure once and for all. It was all no use. Mr. Simmons was steadfast. It was reunion time and Murphy would be fine.

"You can call me on my cell phone and touch base with me in the mornin' to check in on us. I'll have it with me. Don't you worry. If anything happens, you know I'll take him to the closest vet. I just wanted to let you know…we appreciate everything you did for us. I really appreciate you being so thorough and all."

It was a thank you that I didn't deserve. I was frustrated that I had let them both down. It was lose-lose on the Dr. Miller medical scoreboard. Either, I was wrong and should have sent him home initially like grandpa would have, or I should have done a better job of convincing Mr. Simmons to be a no-show at that reunion.

Jen made copies of Murphy's records, lab work, and X-rays. Liz tried to schedule a recheck appointment with Murphy, for when they returned. But Mr. Simmons blew her off, saying he was now a "free man" and didn't know how long he would be staying in Ohio. Assuring us not to worry. He'd let me know when I called him, and "surely set something up."

With that and a 'Thank you to everyone for taking care of Murphy,' Mr. Simmons was gone. I had thought that if Murphy was doing well, it would a be a foregone conclusion that we would see him back after the Simmons family reunion. We didn't know it then but we wouldn't be seeing them for any recheck appointment.

Friday 8:32 am

I went straight for Murphy's record, picked up the phone, and called the cell number.

"You have reached Ron Simmons. Can't get your call now. Leave me a message, and I will get back to you. BEEP."

"Hey, it's Dr. Miller. I just wanted to check in on Murphy. If you could give me a call back when you get a chance. Thanks."

I called Mr. Simmons again that afternoon and that evening. It was the same drill: call, voicemail, and leave a message. I even called from home on Saturday morning. It carried on to the following week. I tried on Monday, Tuesday, and Wednesday morning. When he didn't answer those times I just hung up.

By Thursday, Jen was advising me not to make any more calls. "You can't keep harassing him, Dr. Miller. He obviously knows you are trying to reach him. Even if he didn't, you'd think he'd call here and tell us …something. It's all just weird." Even without her advice, I had been thinking the same thing.

The entire practice was at a loss to explain what had happened. As usual, we had already started thinking about all the negative scenarios. Did we lose Murphy, or perhaps something had happened to Mr. Simmons? Jen was convinced she knew the real answer.

"As usual, Dr. Miller, you know our level of care is too complicated for some of these people. He really needed a vet just like his old one and that's not the way you practice. His little trip was the perfect opportunity for him to make a clean break from us. You gave that dog really good care. I just worry about what happened to the dog. Really, it'd be nice to know…"

I was starting to agree with her and latched on to her explanation. Especially when that explanation would leave them both in good health.

I broke down and wrote one of the only client follow-up letters of my career. Ethically, in cases where you fail to contact a client over results, or a crucial follow-up, it's the last and final move. After which, you are free of any medical responsibility. Of course, it doesn't free you from continuing to want to know what happened. After sending the letter, we waited. Unfortunately, as with the phone calls, he didn't respond. We eventually did get a response and answer to what happened to Murphy. It was from something we never would've suspected would prompt him to contact us.

Just a Little Reminder, Your Pet is Due...

It was well over a year later when we finally heard back from Mr. Simmons. It was actually our computer-generated yearly reminder cards that we send out, which brought him back. When Liz saw his reminder card, she figured that if Murphy was OK, at least Mr. Simmons would know his annual exam was due. Even if he had decided to take Murphy elsewhere.

Like with most of the news in my practice, I was the last one to find out about all this. I was looking over my appointments for the following day when I saw it: *"Simmons, Ron. Murphy. Annual Exam. Owner states is doing well."* It was a definitive WTF moment. I calmly approached Liz in order to ask about this oversight.

"What the hell, Liz? Ron Simmons shows back up on the radar and nobody tells me?! You think *I* might want to know what happened? What the hell is going on in this place!? What did he say!?"

"Calm down, Dr. Miller. I told you about this. I know I did. The computer generated a reminder for his annual months ago. I guess he finally called to get Murphy up-to-date on his shots. He said Murphy was doing great. He didn't really say much, and I didn't want to press him."

Jen, of course, immediately came to Liz's defense and chimed in with, "We all discussed this. Ages ago. You just forgot, and you're just seeing the appointment he made, like weeks ago, today? Really, Dr. Miller? It's been on the computer the whole time. And now you're starting with us? Here we go again, just like everything else we tell you, you forget. Cut Liz some slack. Will you?"

In a last-ditch effort, I turned to Cassey to get some sort of support on this one. But it was no use. She was confused about why I was upset in the first place and freely agreed with Jen and Liz. Outnumbered, by the bond of the technician sisterhood, I was left to apologize. As always to get back on their good side and against my will and better judgment, I ordered them lunch the next day.

Ron Simmons showed back up like nothing happened. That day, he was sporting an untucked white polo shirt, jeans, and black sneakers. This time, he decided to wear his prescription sunglasses the whole appointment. Talking to him with his sunglasses on was the least awkward thing about that appointment.

I wanted to directly ask in the same 'calm' manner I used with Liz, "What the hell happened, Mr. Simmons? Didn't you get my messages? I even sent you a letter. Come on, man, what were you thinking?" My professional judgment, and Mr. Simmons's endearing personality, of course, would never allow that dialog to take place. Instead, I pretended that nothing ever happened. It was still on my mind the whole time and I definitely had my fair share of awkward pauses and stutters talking to Mr. Simmons. He did agree on running Murphy's blood work.

It returned the next day, and it was completely normal. His RBC and platelets were well within normal limits. It confirmed the most likely diagnosis. Murphy had had a minor bleed in his abdomen from his run-in with Mr. Simmons's truck. The bleeding had stopped and eventually his RBC had returned to normal. I never figured out the reason behind Mr. Simmons's lack of response to all my calls and my letter. One thing is for certain. If grandpa had sent this case home, veterinary medicine would have worked out just fine for grandpa. At least for this one, it would have.

It's Complicated

Making key decisions is an integral part of daily life in my practice. Most commonly, it involves changing a treatment plan. That change may be dictated by something simple such as the owner being unable to give pills to their pet, or they need a medication that's less expensive. Things start to get a little more complicated when they can't afford a specific treatment plan, and we need to come up with a medical Plan B. It gets a lot more complicated when there is no Plan B, leaving only the situation that most people hope and pray they never get into with their pet.

Things aren't always clear-cut in the decision-making department. Sometimes we think we made the right decision and hindsight proves otherwise. It's really rough when that right decision leads to the outcome that no one wanted. Whether it's an outcome we could foresee or not doesn't really matter. It's rough either way. Sidney Davis was one of those.

Sidney Davis had the same backstory as many of our feline patients that are adopted as kittens. Either they were found wandering around homeless, or a 'friend' had a cat that wasn't spayed and it magically got pregnant. Regardless, a kitten was down on its luck, needed a home, and they adopted it. In this backstory, Sidney's initial owners also had some bad luck of their own.

Mr. (Officer) Davis was responding to a residential break-in. The family's home was hit during the day, and they arrived home that evening to find out the bad news. Thankfully, the new litter of kittens and their mom were all still safe and sound. The same could not be said for the front door, jewelry, and some of the electronic devices they had lying around. It was on that call, that Officer Davis took a liking to a cute, solid gray male kitten in the litter. He ended up taking it home that night to surprise his wife. It was no surprise to us, however, that she instantly loved that little gray kitten from the start.

When it comes to John and Karen Davis, they are true animal lovers. They're among our best clients. What makes a great client is really simple: they are easy to deal with and follow what we recommend. That's essentially all there is to it. Like all things in life, being set financially always makes things easier. But, despite what people may think, that is not a requirement of being a great client. Lastly, an added bonus of a great client is that their pet is, or pets are, well-behaved. Mr. and Mrs. Davis are all of those things. We even landed the bonus, their English bulldog, Bernie, loves us.

Sidney was another win in their great client category. From the moment we met him, he was the cat patient that every veterinarian dreams of. You could do any procedure you wanted to him without any kind of hassle. He never got bent out of shape. In fact, he'd even nudge you, looking for attention when it was all over. In a lot of respects, his personality was more like a dog than a cat. Some of that may have to do with the fact that Bernie essentially raised Sidney. To say they got along well together would be an understatement. They'd eat together, play together, sleep together, and even get into trouble together. A lot of these moments, Mr. Davis would capture on his iPhone, and then share them with us. However, we got to live through a couple of these magic moments first hand.

"The partners in crime did it again!" Mr. Davis jokingly explained to me in the exam room. That time, Sidney had knocked an open bag of Doritos off the kitchen counter. Bernie made quick work of the bag, and Officer Davis arrived on the scene too late to stop the crime. He wasn't able to save the Doritos or save Bernie from his pending blow out diarrhea. The diarrhea was so bad, we had to hospitalize Bernie on fluids for two days.

There were other times; slices of bread, cookies, and other assorted goodies but those never landed Bernie into the practice. We only ended up seeing Bernie one other time. That time he got diarrhea from a box of donut holes that Sidney knocked off the table. The donut holes weren't as bad as the Doritos, and we were able to treat Bernie on an out-patient basis. Those were both straightforward cases and didn't compare to when Sidney came in several years later. That problem had nothing to do with Bernie and was far more serious and a lot more complicated.

The First Decision

Tuesday 4 pm

It was one of those emergency appointments that Liz immediately tells us about as soon as she gets off the phone. She tells us even before she formally enters it into the computer. This time, she even walked back to the treatment area to deliver the bad news face to face. I had just finished removing the sutures from a recheck spay appointment and came out of the exam room to find Liz explaining it all to Jen and Cassey.

"Mr. Davis just called. It's Sidney. He's been straining to urinate since early this morning. He just vomited, and he's really lethargic. I told him to bring him right over." Liz already had a pretty good idea what was wrong with Sidney. We all did. We always hope we're wrong, especially in this case, but we weren't.

Twenty minutes later, I walked into the exam room with Jen. John Davis was standing over Sidney who was on the exam table. Mr. Davis was still in full uniform. He represented my stereotypical image of a young police officer. He was tall, had a muscular build, and both his arms were covered in tattoos. He gave me the impression that he could handle anything the job could throw at him. His brown hair was buzzed short on the sides and slicked back on the top. I never officially asked him where he's from but I always placed him from being from somewhere in the southwest, like Texas or Oklahoma.

Every time he sees me, without fail, he shakes my hand. Even his handshake was intimidating. His large hand swallowed mine and I felt like a little kid shaking an adult's hand. I always desperately try to save some manhood with my best firm grip but it's a losing proposition. Despite his appearance, he is always laid back, polite, and seems to go out of his way to be friendly.

I could already tell Sidney was in bad shape. He was laying on his side on the exam table, motionless. When Jen gently picked him up to weigh him, he let out a loud cry. Mr. Davis who felt just as bad for Jen, as Sidney, stated, "It's OK he's been crying at home too. He cried out the whole way here."

I dove right into my exam, as I was getting Sidney's medical history. I was anxious to get to the part of his exam that would tell me if it what was what we all feared it was.

"When was the last time you've seen him urinate?" I asked as I made my way through his exam. I knew once I reached his abdomen, I'd have the answer.

"That's the thing, he's been in and out of the litter box all day. He just strains and only produces a few drops. The last time he went... normally, would have been last night. He hasn't eaten at all today. I thought he might have a urinary tract infection (UTI), and I was planning on bringing him in tomorrow. But when he threw up twice, I called. He wasn't this lethargic this morning, he—"

He stopped midsentence when I palpated Sidney's abdomen who'd let out an uncharacteristic horrific scream.

When I felt his abdomen, one component was abnormally large and distended. It was his bladder. It was massive. The size was easily ten times normal. When I felt his bladder, he strained in response and produced several drops of bloody urine. I knew instantly that Sidney was 'blocked.'

A blocked cat is a male cat who can't urinate because their urethra is obstructed. Several things can cause this type of blockage; bladder stones, a plug of mucus from a nasty UTI or an intense spasm from inflammation. In many cases, the cause of the spasm isn't known, AKA it's idiopathic. In medicine, when we don't know what causes something we'll put the fancy label of idiopathic on it. Whatever the cause, a urethral blockage isn't good.

The urine contains all the waste products filtered out of the bloodstream by the kidneys. Once the plumbing gets backed up, the waste products build up in the circulation. Things go downhill from there. Electrolyte and metabolic balances that we take for granted, all get thrown out of whack from this little blockage. This causes a laundry list of issues. The kidneys take the biggest hit but even organs like the heart can be affected and develop an arrhythmia.

All these imbalances have to be addressed. Making things even more complicated, we can't wait to completely fix all those issues because we have to go under anesthesia to deal with that obstruction. When we have a less-than-ideal candidate for anesthesia, that's an 'anesthetic risk.' So, despite the simple mechanism, the treatment is complicated and can be expensive.

Wait, there's more. On average, roughly thirty percent of these cats will return with the same problem. They may even return within a week, or the month after treatment. In other words, they come back blocked (all jacked up again) putting owners through the exact same financial and emotional turmoil as the first time.

For patients whose owners can't afford the supportive care, anesthesia, and hospitalization, there is an alternative medical plan. It's no Plan B because its results are so variable and highly dependent on the type of obstruction. Basically, it revolves around injectable narcotic medications, draining the bladder every eight hours, cystocentesis, and praying the cat urinates on its own. If the patient has high kidney values or a physical obstruction, this medical Hail Mary has basically no chance of working.

As soon as I felt Sidney's bladder, all the blocked-cat scenarios started playing out in my mind. I immediately started to get the all-too-familiar feeling of nervous anxiety. I had been in this situation before. It's always hard to predict how it will end but now, it was Mr. Davis and Sidney. He would have to make a decision on whether to treat Sidney or take an option that nobody likes to think about. At first glance, *that* option may seem heavy-handed and inhumane, but it's not. For many owners, a treatment plan that goes well over three figures, and a potential for relapse is too overwhelming. For them, the difficult decision is, in fact, the right one.

"Sidney is blocked. He can't urinate at all and that's why he's been straining all this time. It's also why he's been sick. It's because all the toxins that are supposed to go out in his urine are building up in his bloodstream." It was my introduction, to a lengthy explanation that would follow.

"I see, poor guy… What do we need to do?" he responded.

I went over all of it with him. The causes, the effects, and the medical game plan. I discussed the diagnostics, dealing with the obstruction, anesthetic risk, and hospitalization. I even got the bad news out of the way about the potential for reoccurrence.

There was a pause as he absorbed everything. Jen, who had taken her usual position against the wall, had been fixated on Mr. Davis the entire time. As with all patients who face a potential final decision she was also anxious to find out what was going to happen. There was no denying that Sidney Davis had a special place in our practice, and he was one of those patients who we all had become (too) attached to. No one was attached to Sidney more than Jen. If it had not been obvious to us all already, it would become even more obvious later on.

"I'd like to see an estimate, just so I know where we are all at. But I can tell you already…we are going to do what we have to do," Mr. Davis replied flatly and without emotion. Similar to my profession, Mr. Davis had become skilled at hiding his emotions in difficult situations. As Jen and I left the exam room, he stood there rhythmically stroking Sidney, with a blank expression on his face.

When Jen went back in with the estimate, Mr. Davis looked at the bottom figure. Without asking any questions, he quickly signed it as if it were simply a formality instead of a consent to proceed with a complicated medical plan.

Jen came out of the exam room cradling Sidney like a baby. I was already calculating his dose of injectable pain medication but just in case I'd forgotten, Jen immediately barked, "Hurry up with a dose, Dr. Miller! It'd be nice to get some pain meds on board for him. How would you feel if you couldn't pee?"

"I've got it! It's right here. Calm down," I said drawing up the medication into the syringe.

As I injected into Sidney's vein, I dropped a "You need to calm down, *Jennifer*" for good measure. Jen, of course, is not a fan of me telling her to calm down (especially twice) or of calling her by her complete first name. Of course, this instigation was not lost on Jen.

"I am calm! Do I look excited? No, I don't. I just look like a good technician who is concerned about your patient. You're lucky you have a crack team like us working with you. Ask Cassey, even she agrees," she stated, holding Sidney, and looked to Cassey who was drawing his blood to get her response.

"I'm not getting involved in all this but I would definitely agree we get the job done. If I was you, Dr. Miller, I'd stop antagonizing her so we can get the lab work and X-rays finished," Cassey chimed in, doing a poor job, as always and on purpose, at trying to stay neutral.

I slid in among them and drained some urine off his bladder with a needle and syringe to get a urine sample and offer him a bit of relief. The real relief would come once I'd addressed his blockage. Jen made the usual comment about me "rudely forcing my way" in the middle of them unannounced, and without prefacing it with an "excuse me." Deciding to take Cassey's advice, I offered my best fake apology as I finished draining Sidney's bladder.

As they promised, they got everything completed in rapid fashion. I hoped we'd catch a break on his blood work but we didn't and things were already going downhill. Like all blocked cats that land in our practice, his kidney values were ridiculously elevated. His X-rays offered us better news; he didn't have any large stones in his urethra or

83

in his bladder. The other piece of good news was his ECG. Aside from his elevated heart rate, it was normal. The last piece of this puzzle was his urine sample. He had the makings of a serious UTI loaded with red blood cells, white blood cells, and a ton of bacteria. In order to confirm it, I sent it to the lab for a culture. In the meantime, I was going to start him on antibiotics.

4:45 pm

I took the lab work and radiographs into the exam room. I went over all the lab work and radiographs we had done. The response from Mr. Davis was all very matter of fact. Even when I explained, that after all was said and done, there was a chance Sidney could return with the same exact problem. He understood and his demeanor remained unchanged. It was as if he'd been through it all before. However, when I started to discuss where Sidney was going to spend the night, his disposition changed slightly.

"It's almost five o'clock now. We are going to stay late and put Sidney under anesthesia to relieve the obstruction. As we discussed, we are going to leave a urinary catheter in place for the next thirty-six hours. After he wakes up from the anesthesia, I'd like to discharge him to the emergency clinic for them to watch him overnight—" Uncharacteristically, he interrupted me.

"Hold up. I thought he'd stay here. Emergency clinic? We've been there before, with Bernie that one time, when he chewed up the baby's pacifier. They are good at what they do and all, and I get it, Doc. Trust me, I get the cost. But they're really expensive, and with what you guys are doing here…I think that may, may price Sidney out of the game. Can't you keep him here? We trust you guys."

In the perfect-world scenario, this cat goes to the emergency clinic. There he gets the minute-to-minute attention in a hospital that is fully staffed all night. I tried to counter with "After the anesthesia, and the urinary catheter and everything…I'd really like them to watch him, at least for tonight."

"I hear you. But, we are going to have to go with him staying here overnight. I'm afraid we don't have a choice..."

I understood and agreed to keep Sidney overnight. It wasn't the ideal situation but I could improvise. We had been in the same situation with other blocked cats before. I promised to call him after Sidney was awake and, with that, Mr. Davis left.

I went back to the treatment area. Sidney already had an IV catheter in his front leg and was on fluids. Getting an IV catheter in cats can sometimes be difficult. With Sidney nothing is ever difficult. Even though he was slightly sedated from his pain injection, even under normal circumstances, we'd get a catheter in just gently restraining him.

Jen and Cassey were rushing around getting ready for Sidney's procedure. My staff are usually all business but when it comes to staying late, they really step their game up. They want to get things done and go. Nobody is excited about staying late. They also aren't too excited about coming in late at night to check on a patient either. Add those two together and it's even worse news. This was the little piece of information I had to fill them in on.

When it comes to deviating from the original medical script, sometimes I end up having to argue both sides of the medical fence. I'm like the politician who has changed his stance and then has to pander for votes on his new crappy position. Now, I had to take the client's position against the view I held myself just moments ago. Primarily it turns into a debate with the most difficult vote to flip, Jen.

Even though Jen lives over thirty minutes away, and that gets her out of doing night checks, it doesn't stop her from joining in with the discussion. She is the most vocal one in expressing everyone's views on having to come in at night. Especially when the patient really should be at the emergency clinic in the first place. I don't know if she is doing her part in standing up for the technician sisterhood, or like with most things, just likes arguing with me. Either way, it always makes delivering bad news painful.

"I understand. They don't want to go to the emergency clinic and spend even more money. I feel bad for them, I really do. I especially feel bad for Sidney. I got this one, guys. I'll check on him. No problem, Dr. Miller. I got this one."

Yeah, that really was Jen's response, and it took me a few minutes to process it. When I eventually figured it out later, the reason was so blatantly obvious I felt dumb for not seeing it from the start. In a profession that involves patients who are helpless, we find ourselves going that extra mile for just about everybody. Once in a while, there is that special pet that you become even more attached to. It could be a breed you have soft spot for, their personality, or sometimes reasons you just can't explain. For Jen, Sidney was one of those patients. She would do almost anything she could to help, even if it meant driving longer than anyone else. As an added bonus she'd do it without complaining.

Minutes later, we had Sidney under anesthesia. Getting a urinary catheter into a blocked cat can be daunting, especially if it's a stone. Those cases are never fun, and sometimes bring along another decision-making process for the owner. If the case is severe enough or there are a number of stones in the urethra, I'll refer it to the specialist as soon as I see the X-ray. This way if the specialist can't move the stones into the bladder, they can take the cat straight to surgery for a urethrostomy. A urethrostomy diverts the urethra to bypass the obstruction. This creates a new opening for a male cat through which to urinate, similar to a female. Sidney's obstruction was just mucous and debris, so it was supposed to be straightforward and easy. It wasn't.

"Dr. Miller, this is catheter number three, make this one count. We only have two left now," Jen quipped referring to two plastic catheters I had already kinked, failing to flush the obstruction. It had only been a few minutes but it had started to feel like a lot longer. I hadn't discussed the 'what if we couldn't get a catheter in' scenario with Mr. Davis.

As I struggled flushing saline and lube into catheter number three, that phone call started to play out in my mind. Of course, in my case, another potential outcome comes to mind. After a complicated referral to the specialist transpires, Sidney is placed under anesthesia yet again. Except, this time, the specialist triumphantly passes a urinary catheter with ease on their very first attempt, leaving everyone to wonder, "What the hell is wrong with that Dr. Miller?"

I didn't have to make that call. Finally, after a few choice expletives, which I reserve for cases just like this, I felt the saline flow from the syringe without resistance. It was a feeling of satisfaction and relief as I advanced that *fourth* catheter freely along Sidney's urethra into his bladder. Instantly, urine flowed from the end of the catheter unobstructed.

Jen applauded my efforts as she turned down Sidney's anesthesia, "Maybe next time we can get this done with fewer than four catheters. You'd figure after all these years you'd have some sort of technique to get this done with just one or two, instead of like… four," she said trying to give me her version of a good-natured hard time.

I sutured his catheter in place and I flushed his bladder several times to remove as much debris as possible. Jen and Cassey made quick work of attaching an extension line, and an empty IV bag to Sidney's urinary catheter, to neatly capture the urine.

5:45 pm

Sidney was recovering in a kennel from anesthesia but wasn't completely awake yet. It was time to call Mr. Davis. As I waited for Mr. Davis to answer, I stared at the line perfectly taped to Sidney's tail and followed it as it draped effortlessly out of the cage and to the fluid bag hung outside below. The ingenious setups my staff devise never cease to impress me, and Sidney's catheter bag was no exception.

Everything looked perfect. The IV fluids, the electronic fluid pump, the urinary bag, his paper e-collar, and even the bed of towels that Jen had personally arranged. It looked like a picture straight from a veterinary journal.

Except in reality, beyond the picture, cats are not humans. They aren't mindful of fluid lines and urinary catheters. Even with the best cat, who is also 'drugged up' on pain meds, having lines running in and out of it is a recipe for disaster. Sometimes, despite our best efforts, really good drugs, or awesome setups, they will manage to pull these lines out.

An IV catheter is easily replaced but a urinary catheter isn't. Aside from the ordeal and the added expense of going under anesthesia a second time, it poses another problem. Replacing a urinary catheter can aggravate the urethra leading to more inflammation and spasms, and negatively impact the outcome of the case. This is why having the emergency clinic babysit these cases is always our first choice.

Mr. Davis answered on what seemed like the very last ring before it would go to voicemail.

"Hey, Doc, I thought I missed you for a second. I was out walking Bernie. He's been pacing all over the house looking for his buddy. I figured I'd try and tire him out. How's ol' Sidney doing by the way?" his voice was friendly and without any type of worry. Either, like most clients, he dismissed the inherent risk of anesthesia I had told him about or was hiding behind his first-responder facade.

"Sidney is not completely awake but we are done with the anesthesia and he's waking up now. I managed to relieve his obstruction and his urinary catheter is in place. We are going to hang out here until he's completely awake. Do you want Jen to give you a call when she checks on him tonight?"

Mr. Davis opted out of having Jen call him with an update, or as we would say took the no-news-is-good-news option.' He told me all about a long shift, a baby that was up all night, and hoping to get some much-needed sleep. So, as long as Sidney was OK we didn't need to call him.

Jen was the first one to leave, taking advantage of our unwritten night-check rule. If you're coming back, you get the early exit. It precludes you from cleaning up and gives the maximum amount of time before having to turn around and come back. Liz and Cassey started to work on cleaning up the disaster of discarded catheters, syringes, veterinary equipment, and other assorted medical wrappers in the treatment area.

Like all good bosses, I pitched in at the beginning but I always play the role of good vet/ horrible technician. It didn't take long before Liz and Cassey got frustrated with the way I do things and pleaded with me to leave. Since Sidney was completely awake, and (despite what she'll tell you) my drive is about just as long as Jen's, I took them up on their offer. On my way out, I mustered up my best thank-you appreciation speech but, based on their responses, I knew I'd have to butter them up with yet another lunch.

11:45 pm

I was well into my slumber when I was awakened with "Who run the world?! Girls! Who run the world?! Girls!" being belted out by Beyoncé. It was the new ringtone I had set for the practice. It had previously been Katy Perry, an inside joke since I have an all-female staff. When Jen found out I associated the staff with Katy Perry, she lectured me about appearing misogynistic. She then took it upon herself to choose my new practice ringtone that would portray the staff in a more positive light.

"Let's face it, Dr. Miller, you know as well as we do that we run this practice," she said, celebrating her selection with the rest of the staff. Making matters worse, she went on to inform me that I'd have a full-on tech mutiny on my hands if ever tried to change it.

After the ringtone startled me out of my sleep, I felt a wave of anxiety come over me. When it comes to night checks, I'm also on the no-news-is-good-news option. Most of the cases we hospitalize are mostly routine so, this works out quite well (for me). I immediately thought something must be wrong with Sidney.

89

"Hey, Dr. Miller, don't worry, Sidney is OK. Both catheters are still in and everything looks good. I'm really sorry to bother you, sir, but you forgot to let me know the dose of pain meds for Sidney."

She was right. It had been an oversight on my part. The staff had written his medication on our whiteboard but I failed to write out the actual dose in the record. At this stage of her vet game, Jen could easily calculate the dose herself but when it comes to a medical issue, she does everything by the book. That responsibility lies with the doctor. Even though she has no problem interfering with business in other areas, that's a line she'd never cross. I quickly scrambled and gave her a dose to keep Sidney comfortable until morning.

"Thanks, sir. I'll go ahead and give him that. Like I said, he looks good...his fluids were running when I got here, and the urinary catheter is still good. So, we're OK here," she explained, referring to another problem we encounter when pets sit on, or kink, their fluid lines.

"That's good news. You had me worried for a second. I'm glad he's doing OK. Thanks for checking on him."

"You're welcome, sir. See you tomorrow."

That exchange would surprise anyone who has met or even worked with Jen briefly. But I know her way better than that. After working with her for over a decade, it was one of her more pleasant idiosyncrasies that I was all too familiar with. Jen has an alter ego, and it likes to use "sir." I confront her on this formality on a regular basis and she always tells me it's because she is a consummate professional. There is some truth to that. However, I have always speculated that the real reason is she has a paranoia that something unprofessional she says on the phone or via text will be recorded and used against her in the future.

After I hung up the phone, I struggled to go back to sleep. I started to worry about Sidney. Would he manage to keep his urinary catheter in? More importantly, would he make it through all this? I managed to convince myself that he'd be fine. Not only would his catheter stay in but his obstruction was relatively simple. It was just a UTI and he'd be fine. It would all work out. It had to, this was Sidney Davis. I finally fell asleep. If I had known the real outcome, I would have been up all night.

Wednesday 8:05 am

Anxious to check on Sidney, I arrived uncharacteristically early. I expected to find Jen there before me and I was right. As I walked into the treatment area, I found her attending to Sidney.

"I gave him all his meds already, sir. I'm just fixing up his bed. Everything is looking good. He even ate this morning," she updated me, still assuming the role of her more formal alter ego.

"You already gave him his meds and he has eaten already?"

"Yeah, Dr. Miller, I was here early. I was worried about him last night. So, I decided to come in at seven. His fluid line was kinked when I got here but, according to the fluid pump he got most of the fluids overnight…so, it must have kinked just before I got here. I changed his urine bag, it had some blood in it, but what's coming through now looks pretty good."

I went over to his kennel and gave Sidney a 'curbside' exam. A curbside exam is a cute term I use to let the techs know I'm doing my exam with the patient in the kennel, or just outside of it. This way they don't have to disconnect the patient from fluid lines or carry any other attached medical goodies to the exam table. Sidney's exam was normal. Despite being hooked up to multiple lines, he was still trying to solicit me for attention throughout his exam.

"Well, Dr. Miller, you can at least pet him. You can tell you're not a cat person," Jen said using the opportunity to remind me, yet again, that I was the only staff member who was cat-less. I complied and rubbed Sidney's head and neck briefly. He instantly started to purr.

91

"That's better, now you look like you *might* be a cat person," Jen proudly stated with a smile, letting me know I had fulfilled my obligations as a cat lover.

I called Mr. Davis. He answered on the second ring.

"I was just thinking about Sidney. How'd he make out overnight?"

"Sidney is doing really well so far. He had some blood in his urine overnight but this morning it's looking quite clear. I'm thinking that if his urine continues to look good, and he does well, I'll probably pull his urinary catheter tomorrow morning. Then it's wait and see on if he urinates OK on his own…"

"I knew he'd be OK with you all. Karen will be happy to hear that, she was kinda worried about ol' Sidney. I'll tell you what, you might as well have called me last night. I was up. Between the baby, and that Bernie, it was a late night. Bernie was pacing, panting, and drooling all over the place. He finally went to sleep. Then the baby woke up crying. Thank God that dog sleeps like he's in coma 'cause if he'd woken up again, he'd probably have started his crazy-ass nonsense all over again. We're both going to need some sleeping pills tonight, Doc, the way this is going. Hopefully, Sidney can come on home tomorrow. I'm off but you can just call me this evening with an update. If something comes up, you can reach me on my cell."

When I got off the phone, I was looking forward to making myself a cup of coffee and getting down to some serious office business at my desk. It had been a while since I'd got to work early, and my first appointment wasn't until nine o'clock. Let's face it, the internet doesn't surf itself. Jen caught on to my plan as soon as she saw me start to brew my coffee.

"Where do you think you're going?" she asked, already knowing the real answer.

"I've got some office work I have to catch up on. You know, like, pay some bills," I tried using my usual cover but, unfortunately, that excuse had died long ago.

"You aren't going to go and play on the internet this morning, Dr. Miller. Your first appointment is already here. So, you can forget about all that. It's Mrs. Sweet, you should know better."

Even though it was barely twenty after eight, Mrs. Sweet had already arrived. Jen was right, I should have known better. She never arrives at her actual appointment time but I thought I could get lucky and grab at least a ten-minute break. As soon as I took the first sip of coffee, I could hear her through the exam-room door talking way too loudly to Liz.

"Ralphie has been digging at his ear all night! I couldn't sleep with all that racket. Let me tell you, dear, when you get to be my age, sleep is a very precious commodity."

The exam-room door opened and Liz backed out through the door saying, "I hear you, Mrs. Sweet. I'm the same way. I need my sleep and my coffee. That's what keeps me going." She handed the record off to Jen. One thing is for sure, when it comes to an exit strategy, no one can beat Liz. Anyone else could have easily been trapped with Mrs. Sweet for a good ten minutes.

Jen took a look at the chart. "Let's go, Dr. Miller. This is a self-check-in. Don't keep me in there this time either. Treat 'em and street 'em. You got me?"

Mrs. Sweet is always a self-check-in. Rather than the techs going in and getting a patient history before me, I rescue them from the quicksand discussion that occurs with Mrs. Sweet. We do the appointment together to try and save time. Despite our best efforts, we aren't always as lucky as Liz.

I went into the exam room and Mrs. Sweet was sitting on the bench resting one hand on her three-pronged cane. Under her arm was her little brown toy poodle, Ralphie. To say Mrs. Sweet is a poodle fan or lover, would be a gross understatement. She is obsessed with her dogs and like most of our clients, she loves them like they're her children. I have always said to staff and clients alike, if we didn't understand that, we'd be in the wrong building.

Having said that, Mrs. Sweet definitely has her own unique pet-owner qualities. The one that never gets old is her gear. Every time we see her, she has a piece of clothing with a poodle on it. I have no idea how she finds it all because I know for a fact she doesn't own a computer or know how to go online. Today was no exception. She had on a dark-blue T-shirt, with a white poodle on it. The poodle was dressed up with a crown, cloak, and made out to be holding a scepter. In the background was a British flag, and on top, in bedazzled letters, it said, "God Save the Queen!"

Jen made short work of getting the appointment underway. As soon as I said hello to Mrs. Sweet, Jen immediately said, "Good morning, Ralphie," and gently took him from her, and placed him on the exam table. Jen made the first mistake by just trying to be polite and asking Mrs. Sweet how she was doing.

"Terrible! This dog has kept me up all night. All he does is dig at that right ear. He went to the groomer three weeks ago. I swear every time he goes, it seems like three weeks later he gets an ear infection. I tell you what, Doctor, that groomer has to go!" Of course, aside from him going there three weeks ago, none of that was true. Anytime one of Mrs. Sweets three poodles gets a skin or an ear infection, the groomer takes the fall. The good news is she's had the same groomer since I've known her.

As I examined his ears, she went on to explain how the groomer was slowly pricing herself out. His left ear was completely normal, but his right ear was inflamed and had a lot of black waxy debris. Despite his ear being sore and uncomfortable, all Ralphie did to object to my otoscope was to try and tilt his head.

The entire time I was describing the infection to Mrs. Sweet, he was enthusiastically trying to lick my hand. Of all her poodles, Ralphie was by far the sweetest. He never protested to anything we did and would go out of his way to try and lick us. He's the complete polar opposite to one of her other poodles, Cuddles, who we have to muzzle to even look at.

"His left ear is normal but you're right about this ear. His right ear has an infection. There is a lot of nasty wax in that ear. We're going to take this sample and look under the microscope to get an idea of what's going on." As soon as I removed the cotton swab from his ear, Jen grabbed the long end of it from me. Aside from being good at what she does, she knew that the cotton swab was her exit strategy out of that exam room. Jen wasn't going to take any chances on letting me use it and leaving her behind.

"I'll take that for you, Dr. Miller." Jen held the swab in one hand and gently handed Ralphie back to Mrs. Sweet. Jen quickly scurried out of the exam room. Thankfully, Ralphie had started licking Mrs. Sweet's face. He was overly excited to be back in her lap. I used the distraction to my advantage and excused myself to go check on the sample.

Jen made quick work of preparing the microscope slide with the cotton swab. Within moments she had the results. "Yeast plus, Cocci plus, plus. Let us know what meds you want, so we can get it going. *I'll* go back in there and show you how it's done. If you go in there to get him, it will be an hour-long production."

Jen went into the exam room with the results and game plan for Ralphie. Within moments she returned with him.

"Told you. That's how you do it," she bragged to me as Cassey cleaned Ralphie's ear.

Ralphie's treatment was straightforward; some ointment for his ear and a twenty-four-hour steroid injection to calm down the inflammation. The injection would buy some time until the combination ointment kicked in. The best part of the ointment was that it would last a week. It would preclude Mrs. Sweet from having to medicate his ear. I like to think of that medication as 'the gift that keeps on giving.' It guarantees the treatment isn't going to get missed on a daily regimen at home, and it helps Mrs. Sweet. I know living alone and being older can make daily ear treatments rough.

After they put the medication in his ear, I gave him his steroid shot. As with everything else, he was an angel of a patient. I led the way and we returned to the exam room.

"He's all done, Mrs. Sweet."

"You already gave him his shot? "

"Yes, he's all done. We cleaned his ear and gave him his first treatment. You don't need to do anything. If he continues to itch or isn't doing well, call me. If he does OK, we'll see him next week."

"Doctor, Jen was telling me all about that medication. That really is fantastic. It makes my life so much easier. You are so advanced with this new medication. How wonderful you all are. Come here..."

She extended her arms signaling me it was time for a hug. I bent down, and she leaned forward from her seat and gave me a hug. It was an awkward position to begin with but it was made even more awkward by her cane caught in between us. As she squeezed me in her embrace the large handle inadvertently jabbed me in my stomach.

After it was finished, she quickly, and without warning, planted a kiss on my cheek. Caught off guard, and feeling my face start to flush, I awkwardly started to explain that the medication was relatively new.

Jen was still holding Ralphie and was anxious to conclude the appointment. When I paused briefly, she interjected, "Come on, Mrs. Sweet, I'll take you up front. Don't worry, I got Ralphie. I'll help you both to the car." She helped Mrs. Sweet to her feet.

After Mrs. Sweet went through the door, Jen turned and winked at me. It was a signal, the exchange she just witnessed would most likely be shared with the entire staff sooner rather than later.

I quickly went to the bathroom to wash the perfect outline of lipstick off my cheek. Thankfully, by the time Jen had returned back from helping Mrs. Sweet, she didn't mention what she'd witnessed moments earlier. Instead, she was busy keeping score with Cassey on how Mrs. Sweet, yet again, managed to stuff a crumpled dollar bill into her hand. I waited all day for the moment she'd drop the hammer one me but, fortunately, it never came.

5:05 pm

Sidney had made it through another day without any issues. I called Mr. Davis to give him the update. "Sidney did great today. He's eating and his urine looks normal. So far, he's doing better than I expected. I'm going to run his blood work in the morning. If everything looks good, I'll probably pull his urinary catheter. Then, it's wait and see if he urinates on his own."

"That's great, Doc. It sounds like you got it all under control over there. If it's OK with you, I think I'm going to do that no-news-is-good-news deal-lio. My shift starts at 5:30 tomorrow morning and, hopefully, everyone actually sleeps tonight. I'll call you in the morning to check in on ol' Sidney."

After I got off the phone, I started to go over the night-check plan with Cassey. As soon, as I started reviewing the medication, Jen interrupted me.

"In case you wanted to know, I'm the one actually doing night check. Make sure you get everything you want listed. That is unless you want me to call you again. I wouldn't want to interrupt your precious beauty rest," Jen sarcastically informed me, a far cry from the apologetic alter ego who'd called the night before. Normally night check is rotated but Jen had insisted on doing it again because it was Sidney. After reviewing everything, I left. At that point, we were convinced that not only wouldn't I be called but that Sidney would do great. It turned out, we were all wrong about everything.

That Next Decision

11:24 pm

"Who run the world?! Girls! Who run the world?! Girls!" Beyoncé woke me up again. I immediately knew it was going to be bad news even before I heard Jen's voice.

"Sorry to wake you, sir, but I got some, some not-so-good news… Sidney is OK and everything but his urinary catheter is kinked really bad. It's pretty much hanging out. It looks like there is a spot of urine on the towel…so he might be urinating. I can't really tell…"

I was hoping the catheter would make it until my arbitrary thirty-six-hour mark. According to the textbook, forty-eight hours is the recommended average duration for an indwelling urinary catheter. For Sidney, I didn't know when his catheter got jacked up but I knew it had been in for at least twenty-four hours.

There was no debate on whether to place another catheter or call Mr. Davis. The wait and see if he urinates was starting tonight. "Do you think he'll let you clip the sutures?"

With any other cat, it would've been ignorant to even ask. So ignorant, that Jen might have even broken from her usual telephone character. There are just two simple sutures but they are in a sensitive area.

"No problem, sir. I'm sure he'll let me do it. I figured you were going to have me do that. If you want, I can put the phone down, and go ahead, and have you hold on. It will only take me a minute…"

Before I could answer she was gone. I could hear her talking to Sidney in the background. I was listening intently, worried that there was a chance he could uncharacteristically scream and explode.

"It's all done, sir. No problem. It was easy, he is so good. What about his IV fluids?"

It was a good question and one I was already considering. If he was urinating, then the fluids would help further flush his bladder and continue to help lower his kidney values. However, if his urethra were to spasm, or he became obstructed we'd be loading up his bladder again.

"Did he eat?"

"Yeah, sir, he ate everything. He looks really bright…"

"Go ahead and take him off fluids. We'll leave his IV catheter in. As soon as you get in tomorrow, go ahead and run his blood work…"

"Sir, the blood work will be waiting for you when you get in. How many years have I been doing this?" It was a rhetorical question but, for the record, Jen has been a tech for over twenty years. And she is excellent at what she does. She actually has been a tech longer than I have been a vet. Those facts aren't lost on Jen, and it's something she likes to remind me about in one way or another.

"Don't worry, sir. I'll also not forget to give him a litter box. Anything else?"

"Nope, you got it all covered. Thanks for checking on him again. I'll see you tomorrow."

"See you tomorrow, sir. Blood work will be up when you get here. Goodnight, sir."

I had trouble falling back asleep. I was already anticipating the worst-case scenario. I would have to call Mr. Davis with bad news and relive the decision process of a second urinary catheter. Not to mention that relapsing and placing a second catheter could equate to a worse prognosis for Sidney. It took me a while to convince myself that Jen had in fact seen urine on his towel and Sidney would be fine. I fell back asleep.

Thursday 8:10 am

I woke up even earlier than on Wednesday but traffic got the better of me. I was stuck behind a geriatric couple on a big motorcycle towing a baggage cart that matched their motorcycle. They were driving way too slow and I couldn't find space to pass on the one-lane road. I couldn't wait any longer. I broke down and called the practice so I could get the answer. Just like the staff, I never call unless it's important. Liz read the caller ID and knew exactly why I was calling.

"Good morning, Dr. Miller. Let me get you over to Jen. I think his blood work should be up. He did urinate overnight, by the way. Hold on."

Jen answered. "Well, well, Dr. Miller. Couldn't get out of bed this morning eh, sir. Just think about me, I actually had to come in last night. Don't worry about us here or anything. His blood work was completely normal. He's urinating like a champ. You can tell this cat wants to go home. He's been pacing in his kennel and crying at me to pet him."

"That is awesome news. Man, I was starting to worry about him."

"So, now that you don't have to rush in, how about picking us up some bagels, muffins, or sum-thin'. I think after all this you kind of owe us. Wait—" she paused and I could hear her talking with Cassey in the background. "OK, yeah, good point. According to Cassey, you still owe them lunch for your weak cleanup job. Nice, Dr. Miller. A supposed great practice owner who doesn't even know where stuff goes in his own practice...after how many years? Sad. Really sad. Well, we all decided on bagels. Later!"

8:49 am

Everyone loves a free lunch. They also love a free breakfast, which is why I didn't hear any complaints when I walked in late with a bag of fresh bagels.

"Good morning, sir. Your first appointment just got here so you're fine. I'll go ahead and get this stuff all spread out, while you and Cassey bang out that annual. Thanks for the bagels," Jen said to me as she traded the record for the bag. It felt like I was getting the short end of that trade, while Jen was getting first dibs on the bagels just like she does with everything else.

When I finished the cat annual, I headed straight for the bagels. It wasn't the elaborate set up that Jen had made it out to be. It consisted of the crumbled-up paper bag of bagels, next to the open cream-cheese container with a plastic knife stuck in the middle. I had just started to open the bag when Liz came over the speakerphone.

"It's Mr. Davis on line one."

I left the fancy spread and picked up the phone.

"How's old Sidney doing? You take the catheter out yet?"

"Sidney beat us to that last night. When Jen came in for night check, his urinary catheter was kinked and pretty much out, so we pulled it. He's been urinating OK so far. We also already ran his blood work and it's completely back to normal."

"That's really great news, Doc. I know Bernie is going to be happy to have his buddy home. I didn't take any chances last night. I took big Bernie on a long walk to tire him out. Then I moved his bed into the laundry room. I don't know if he freaked out again last night but when I went to walk him early this mornin', that sucker was in his bulldog coma. Man, I tell you that dog doesn't wake up for nothin'. You think we'll be able to take him home tonight?"

"As far as he's concerned, he's ready to go right now. He's been crying and pacing in his cage all morning. I'd like to keep an eye on him a bit longer but, if you guys want, he can go home after lunch."

"He's probably trying to get more food out of you all. That's how he plays us at home. I think Karen should be able to swing in there at two. Will that work?"

"Yeah, two o'clock, that, should, work…"

Cassey instinctively picked up my cue. She nodded her head in agreement, as she stood in front of the computer and entered the appointment.

Sidney went all day without any problems. Periodically, he'd call out for attention and rub up along the bars of his kennel. Jen couldn't help herself and would either lean inside his kennel to pet him or offer him a bite of cat food. As for me, it wasn't until eleven o'clock that I finished my appointments and finally got to eat that bagel.

2:04 pm

When Karen Davis showed up that afternoon it turned out to be a production. As she came into the practice, we could hear her infant screaming all the way back in the treatment area. Liz didn't waste any time putting her into the exam room. The baby's crying got progressively louder, and we received a final loud blast, as Liz backed through the exam-room door.

"Thank you so much for the brownies, Karen. I'll need to work out extra hard for these tonight. Dr. Miller will be in in a sec."

Liz was never what I'd call out of shape. But, for some reason, she had just started her new health kick. She seemed to tell anyone and everyone about it, including lecturing us about our current food choices. Jen has been using this "change" to constantly harass me about how I needed to update Liz's picture on our practice website. She claims, Liz has now transformed herself and I need to recognize it. I figured her headshot would look exactly the same; showing her bobbed brown hair, green eyes, and plastered perfect smile. So, even though I always agree with them, I still haven't changed it.

I didn't waste any time going into the exam room. I grabbed all of Sidney's medicine, and 'go home' instructions. I went straight into the exam room and went past Liz as she held the door open. Karen Davis was sitting on the exam-room bench. Next to her, in his car seat, was

103

Kyle Davis. His crying had subsided because Karen was holding a pacifier in his mouth.

Karen Davis was in her early thirties. She had her jet-black hair cut short and parted on the side. Unlike her husband, her accent was bland and I could never figure out exactly where it was from. She was tall and looked just like a runner. I don't know if she still ran but she always showed up in sneakers, athletic shorts, and some sort of T-shirt from a charity run. That day was no exception, and she was in her typical running gear.

"Sorry about Kyle, Dr. Miller. I had to wake him from his nap. I thought he'd go back to sleep on the ride over here, but no dice."

"That's OK. You're fine, I have got kids myself, I completely understand. Wait till he gets on the iPhone. Thank you so much for the brownies. I hope there are some left by the time I get back there," I joked.

I started to go over Sidney's medications, I was about halfway through when Kyle spit out his pacifier and started screaming again. Karen had taken a break from holding it in place, and he had taken the opportunity to spit it out.

I had been in this situation all too many times before, with kids of all ages. It always makes discharges difficult, and I wonder just how much of the stuff I say actually gets absorbed. Sensing I was losing my audience, I wrapped things up, and felt myself rushing through. I was competing with Kyle for her attention and I was losing.

"We're sending him home on a prescription canned urinary diet. I also want you to add an extra litter box. The rule is at least one litter box per cat, plus one extra. As long as he does well, I'd like to recheck him in two weeks." I rushed through the rest, continuing to get interrupted by Kyle's crying.

Jen came through the door with perfect timing. She had Sidney in his carrier and his case of food under her arm.

"Mrs. Davis, those brownies are fabulous. Thank you so much. They were so good, I didn't waste any time. I had to try a bite. Once Dr. Miller gets a hold of those they aren't going to last."

"Thank you, guys, for taking such good care of Sidney. It felt so empty without him. Bernie was a wreck."

"You're welcome, Mrs. Davis, Sidney is one my favorite patients actually. I have to admit, I'm going to kind of miss taking care of him. It was my pleasure. Let me help you to the car with everything…" Jen replied following behind her.

After they left, I immediately started my scavenger hunt for the brownies. It was no surprise that they were already hidden. Fortunately, they always use the same tired location, inside the microwave. When Jen returned, I triumphantly stated, "Those brownies *are* really good" as I took my last bite.

"Dr. Miller, I know you think we hid those brownies but we just keep them in the microwave to keep them fresh."

Friday

I called on Friday when the culture came back confirming he had a UTI. I told Mrs. Davis the results and that it confirmed we had chosen the right medication

"It looks like it! I can't tell you how happy we are to have Sidney back. Especially Bernie," she replied.

On Saturday morning I called again, this time from home. Apparently, I had caught Officer Davis preoccupied with a crime already in progress. He sounded out of breath when he answered the phone.

"Hey, Doc. Thanks, thanks for calling. I'm gonna be short with you 'cause Sidney just knocked the damn cereal box over and Bernie's already trying to eat it all up. No! Bernie! Damn it, Bernie! Doc, Sidney is doing awesome. I gotta go—"

I didn't bother to call them again on Sunday. I had already reached the point, in my mind, where his case was essentially over. He would require the routine follow-up but he was out of the woods. Most cats that develop Sidney's problem are from multi-cat households, where stress, and competition for the litterbox are part of their daily life. Sidney seemed far removed from all that. A chance of a relapse was now unlikely. Throughout the week, the more current cases, clients, and patients consumed my thoughts. I forgot all about Sidney.

That Next Thursday

When I came in on Thursday, I could tell by Jen's, uncharacteristically, silent greeting that something was wrong. She looked at me and helplessly pointed to the computer. When I saw the appointment, it felt like a knot in the pit of my stomach.

> *"9:00 AM Emergency appointment. Davis, Sidney. Crying all night. In and out of the litter box. Not Urinating. Lethargic. Not eating."*

I was devastated. I started to scramble back through the case. Wondering what I'd missed, and what could have caused it to go wrong.

"Dr. Miller, what do you think happened? Liz just spoke to them on Monday and they said he was doing fine. I just don't get it. This really sucks," Jen asked, hoping I'd have an answer or some sort of genius plan. I didn't have an answer or a plan.

"Do you think they'll go for putting another catheter in?" Cassey reluctantly asked.

"For Sidney? I'm pretty sure they'll do anything. This is Sidney Davis."

It was a good thing that Jen answered before me. I wasn't as convinced. For the next twenty minutes, as we waited for Mr. Davis to show up, we had already become resigned to the fact that he'd treat

106

Sidney again. Jen even started to set up for us to put in another catheter.

8:58 am.

Instead of allowing Liz to hand me the record, I grabbed it from her and rushed into the exam room. Jen had followed immediately behind me. The scene was almost identical to the week before. Sidney was lying on his side on the exam table. Mr. Davis was in his uniform and stood methodically stroking him. There was one difference that became obvious to me immediately. This time Mr. Davis couldn't use his inherent skills to hide his emotion. He was upset. He was trying his best to hide it, by looking down at Sidney but I could see it.

Jen slid in, to help hold Sidney for his exam.

I started, "Mr. Davis, I can't believe he's relapsed like this. I really was convinced he was out of the woods. He was doing so well. When did this all start?" As I waited for his answer, I immediately started feeling his abdomen.

I was hoping that it would be normal, and when I squeezed it, urine would flow out quite freely. It would prove his UTI wasn't responding to the antibiotics for some reason and he wasn't actually obstructed. It would be the good news we were all looking for. It would be the good news they all deserved, especially Sidney.

I felt his abdomen it was the size of a large orange. His bladder was extremely distended. When I gently squeezed it, Sidney strained in response, and let out a small cry. Then he only managed a produce a solitary drop of bloody urine.

"He was doing great. He's been getting all his meds and everything. Karen even got two extra litter boxes and everything. I just don't get it, Doc. What happened?" Mr. Davis asked looking me straight in the eye.

I didn't have the answer. He shouldn't have been back. We had seen cases that were more complicated, with little or no chance of pulling through, make it. I struggled to find an explanation but couldn't. I already knew the options but I was reluctant to present them because I was afraid to hear the answer. I avoided his gaze and diverted my attention to Sidney.

"He's obstructed again. I'd recommend putting another urinary catheter in and hospitalizing him again…" Just saying it made my stomach knot up again. I knew the prognosis would likely be worse now. I continued, "Ideally, we could refer Sidney to the specialist. He really shouldn't have relapsed and I can't explain why. I'd like to get a second opinion. They'll also monitor him closely overnight like the emergency clinic—"

He cut me off and gave me the response I had feared most. Unfortunately, I had been expecting it since I first saw his appointment that morning.

"Look, Doc, I talked it all over already with Karen…" he paused, again trying to hold back any emotion. "We talked it over and we decided…to put him to sleep. I just can't take him to the specialist or go through all that again. If you or they could guarantee they'd fix all this, maybe… but we just can't swing it for him. I'm sorry."

He looked down. I picked up on what he was alluding to instantly. Not only was it a financial decision but with no guarantees that we could resolve Sidney's issue, it was one I completely understood. I looked over at Jen, and I could see her eyes starting to well up with tears.

I had been through this all too many times in my career but that time I felt lost. I knew whatever I was about to say would do little to help the situation or make anyone feel better. We all stood in silence for several moments, until I started talking again. "We understand, Mr. Davis. I feel horrible for you all. I don't think anyone expected to be blindsided like this. I know how important Sidney is to you all. For what it's worth… I support your decision. You're right. No one can guarantee that this won't happen again, days, weeks, or even months from now. I've seen it happen that way before. I think you've done what we asked…and gave Sidney a solid chance. I understand your decision now. I think we all do."

After another long period of silence, I excused myself, to get the consent form. Cassey who had been listening through the door had already printed it out and handed it to me. I decided to wait a few moments in order to buy some time to suppress my own emotions. I handed him the form and he pulled a ballpoint pen from his pocket instantly before I could offer him mine.

"Dr. Miller, Mr. Davis would like to stay with Sidney. I told him, I'm going to take Sidney back and put a catheter in. Then we can all do it in here together." It was Jen's way of politely giving me the signal that Mr. Davis had chosen 'to be present.' Knowing Mr. Davis, I had already guessed he would be in the majority of owners who elect to stay.

Jen and Cassey made short work of getting an IV catheter in. I went back to the room with Jen. This time she brought Sidney back in on a small pet bed. Mr. Davis stroked Sidney's head, and then bent down and kissed it. He whispered in his ear and stood back up. When he looked me in the eyes, I could see tears forming as he nodded.

I took his cue and slid in next to Jen. The injection was instantaneous. As soon as I finished giving it, Sidney drifted off to sleep for the last time. Mr. Davis continued to stroke Sidney. I took my stethoscope out and listened to his chest but could only hear Mr. Davis's hand against Sidney. "He's gone," I whispered to Mr. Davis, who patted Sidney's head one last time.

"Do you want some time alone with—" Before I could finish, Mr. Davis shook his head no. I made my way around Jen. I wanted to console Mr. Davis and a hug was absolutely warranted. It was a tough decision that no one wanted to make. As two men, trying to hide their emotions, I knew I might be asking for trouble. Mr. Davis is a foot taller than me and much larger in size.

As I approached him he turned to face me, but he faced me at an angle. Instead of extending both arms, he only extended one. We stood in a side-to-side embrace. I ended up practically hugging his waist, as he grabbed my shoulder and squeezed it. After it was over and I went to disengage, my stethoscope got hooked in the wire for his shoulder radio. Thankfully, I noticed it instantly and was able to unhook it without leaving it behind.

Mr. Davis then spoke softly, just above a whisper. "I just wanted to thank you all… for everything. For taking such good care of him… Thanks." He then turned and grabbed the doorknob in what seemed like one motion. He quickly exited, leaving Jen and me behind. Jen was also trying to hide her emotions but the tears had already started to stream down her cheeks. When she caught me staring at her, she quickly scooped up Sidney and left the room.

The treatment area was silent. We were all devastated and at a loss for words. I felt I'd failed as a veterinarian and was still struggling to find an answer. I was hesitant to say anything, worried that as soon as I started to talk, someone would lose it, and I would follow suit.

We all kept silently busy. I was writing up Sidney's record for the last time. Cassey was busy getting Sidney prepared. Jen was on the phone, calling in a favor to have Sidney picked up immediately. Jen didn't want the Davis's to wait to have Sidney's ashes returned back and was expediting the entire process.

When she hung up the phone, I continued to look at his record hoping she would leave us all in silence. It was obvious we were all moments away from losing it and falling apart at the seams. Jen broke the silence. Instead of sending us all over the edge, she rescued us instead.

"Dr. Miller, don't take this the wrong way but, seriously, at the next continuing ed. meeting, you should see if they have some sort of course …some sort of course on hugging or somethin'. In the last week, I have witnessed two of the most awkward hugs that I have ever seen in my life! I felt uncomfortable just watching you. You seriously need some work."

Hello, Newman!

In the veterinary community, there's a prevailing opinion that any pet we own should be adopted or rescued. Purchasing a purebred pet, as a veterinary team member, is definitely looked down upon by these veterinary do-gooders. Coming face to face with these individuals before, I can tell you first hand that once they get wind of your purebred purchase, you'll be branded immediately. Your only chance to get back in their good graces would be to acquire at least one token rescue pet. Personally, I feel I do my part on daily basis to help animals and give back to the community. That doesn't mean I haven't had a few rescues myself but I don't feel the overwhelming requirement to limit my selection solely to abandoned pets.

When I got my purebred English bulldog, I officially paid for him. There was no guilt involved when I cut that check. However, there is no doubt in my mind that I did, in fact, rescue him. As far as owners are concerned, he won the jackpot. Especially compared to the shady characters he could have wound up with. Of course, he wasn't the only one who won the jackpot on that deal.

Sometime in July 2005

It was one of those appointments that slips through the cracks and wasn't supposed to be made in the first place: "New Client. Pregnancy check. English bulldog, Bred six weeks ago." Under normal circumstances, a new client that's a breeder, who also has a bulldog that is already pregnant, is definitely an appointment that I try to avoid. This particular appointment, was a friend or a relative, of a great client. This fact forced me to see it against my better judgment.

When it comes to breeders, in our practice, there are two kinds that we generally come across. The first kind is open to veterinary advice, takes great care of their pets and tries their best to do right by them. The second kind is so good that they know more than the veterinarian. Therefore, they don't need any veterinary advice. They do the bare minimum for their pets and have usually entered the breeding world as a new financial enterprise. The sole purpose of veterinary visits for them is for medical services they can't do themselves at home. This appointment had all the makings of the second kind of breeder.

Before a dog is pregnant, we like to make sure they are up-to-date on vaccines and are in good health before they are even bred. English bulldogs are a breed that MUST have a caesarian section to deliver their puppies. Because of their disproportionately large head, the chance of complications during whelping are so high, cesareans are promptly scheduled in advance. So, it's a really good idea to sort of have an established relationship with the owner before we get to the 'Pregnant English bulldog' phase of the program.

None of that really phased my technician at the time, Chrissy. When it came time to go into that exam room that day, Chrissy was really excited. Chrissy's personality was the complete polar opposite of Jen's. A prime example that opposites do attract, they were close friends. As far as the practice was concerned, Chrissy's upbeat personality was the perfect balance for Jen. Unfortunately, we eventually lost Chrissy to her overly long commute. Our practice and Jen managed to survive without her even though our balance in that department has been slightly off ever since.

"Be positive, Dr. Miller. You love English bulldogs! They're like your favorite breed?" Chrissy overenthusiastically stated, trying to comfort me. To me, her appearance always matched her energetic upbeat personality. She was short, always had her black hair in a ponytail, and her face was peppered with freckles.

Chrissy was right, I have an affinity for English bulldogs. Despite their numerous genetic medical issues, they're all generally affable and very entertaining. For the most part, they make pretty good patients. Their owners are also usually good clients.

Anya Chebyshev, however, wasn't one of those usually good clients When I walked into the exam room she was staring down at her cell phone. She had jet black hair down to her shoulders. I guestimate she was in her early twenties. She wore ripped jeans and a flannel button-down shirt. Her nose was pierced, and she spared no expense on the eyeliner. If she was going for the goth look that day, she'd hit it out of the park.

She completely ignored me when I greeted her and ignored me again when I tried to get a history. Smartphones hadn't burst onto the scene yet but she was preoccupied with the keyboard of her flip phone. It wasn't until the third time that I got a response.

"No, Doctore, no medical issues. Gucci is very healthy. Last vaccine for her two years ago. I do not believe in too many vaccines. I'm here to check if she's pregnant. That's it." Her Eastern European accent was obvious from the start.

Chrissy sensing that the appointment was off to a rough start, tried to divert my attention to Gucci. "You ready for us, Gucci? Good girl!" she overenthusiastically stated, rubbing her head.

Chrissy knelt down to hold her, encouraging me to move on to the exam portion of the program. Gucci was all brown, except for a white head. She was very sweet, and despite desperately trying to lick Chrissy during the exam stood perfectly still. Her exam was normal. But her abdomen was grossly distended and it was obvious she was most likely pregnant.

"How long ago was she bred?" After I asked, it seemed like Chrissy and I stared at Anya for a good minute before she looked up again from her phone.

"I told receptionist. Should be on your record. About six weeks ago. I have this date written at home."

Pregnancy in dogs lasts on average sixty-three days. Puppies will show up on ultrasound at around twenty-eight days, and on X-ray at forty-five days. Ultrasound can determine early pregnancy and give us information on fetal vitality. Unfortunately, it is cost-prohibitive for many owners.

113

An X-ray, on the other hand, is a lot less expensive. We consider one X-ray to be safe to Mom and her litter. Ideally, we would do both but, in an effort to streamline economic practicality, one X-ray after six weeks is the standard for most owners.

When I went over the estimate with Anya for the X-ray, fecal test, and heartworm test her eyes never left her phone. She brushed us along with a wave. "Yes, go. Fine. Do all dis," she answered like we were her lower-level employees and had bothered her with a question we should have known the answer to.

Gucci's X-ray amazed me when I saw it. I counted several times in disbelief but it was apparent that there were at least ten puppies. It was one of the largest bulldog litters I had ever seen. On average, most bulldog litters I have come across have about four.

As I shared the X-ray news with Anya, she looked up from her phone briefly as I counted the puppies pointing each one out with my pen. She managed to crack a smile but by the time I went over the negative heartworm and fecal test she was back on the keyboard. Needless to say, my efforts to get her to schedule a C-section fell on deaf ears.

After she left, Liz buzzed back on the speakerphone, "She said she'll call us after she looks at her schedule." Of course, that call never came. We all figured she would try to find some less expensive veterinarian to do it, or Gucci would end up as an emergency C-section somewhere. Like many fly-by appointments, we had forgotten all about her for a while. That is until Gucci Chebyshev appeared back on the appointment schedule. None of us could believe what the appointment actually said, so we made Liz personally explain it.

Anticipating this, Liz gave us her prepared speech. It was obvious she wasn't too happy that we doubted her appointment-making skills. "Yes! It's to examine her and the puppies. And, yes, she whelped them all naturally. I didn't believe it all myself but that's what she said. You were right Dr. Miller, there were ten. She says that they are all doing well. OK?!"

Jen and I were convinced that something was missing from that story, like a C-section somewhere. We figured Anya was smart enough to know that we wouldn't see a patient back who'd had a C-section at another practice. If it had been done at the emergency clinic they would have faxed us the report as their primary vet, and that report never came.

Jen started her daily mantra all the way up until the appointment. "She better bring Gucci in with those puppies. If that dog has an actual incision, we aren't looking at any puppies! Period. She can go back to the doctor who did it!"

Jen had insisted she would go into the exam room with me for that appointment. She was concerned that after seeing all those cute puppies, I'd sell out and hesitate to promptly boot Anya from the practice. Especially if I was in there with Chrissy. Despite her best efforts, Jen never made it into the exam room that day. She was in a meeting with a pharmaceutical rep., and it went into overtime. Chrissy stepped in instead. I can't say for certain but had Jen been in that exam room the outcome might have been completely different.

Monday, August 15

The exam room looked like a disaster area. A load of crumpled paper towels and tissues were strung out all over the exam room. An empty coffee cup rested on the exam table. Almost every cabinet had been left open. On the floor, I could see several streaks of bloody postpartum discharge, and puddles of drool everywhere. Judging from the mess, it looked like a failed attempt at a cleanup job.

It never ceases to amaze me how certain clients can generate that much trash in a period of just a couple of minutes while waiting. Most individuals could clean the entire exam room with a quarter of the supplies Anya had used. It was also no surprise that, like many clients, she had opened every single cabinet except the one with the garbage can.

In the corner of the room was a large laundry basket loaded with newborn English bulldogs. All of them seemed to be whining for their mommy. Gucci was frantically drooling and pacing between Anya and the basket. Anya, who seemed oblivious to everything, was sitting and frantically typing on the flip phone.

Chrissy and I made short work of cleaning up the crumpled paper towels and tissues. I personally discarded the coffee cup. I greeted her when we walked in but she chose to wait until we'd finished cleaning up to acknowledge me.

"Hello, Doctore. We had quite a productive weekend. Sorry about dis mess but I could not find your secret garbage can—"

Chrissy immediately went to the basket of puppies and interrupted her with, "They are so cute!" She took one puppy out and held it up. Before she could take it over to the exam table, I motioned her to put it back and pointed at Gucci. I was anxious to examine her. I had to see the C-section incision for myself. I was also curious how Anya would play off the obvious lie she had told us.

I raced through her exam. Even as I listened to her heart, I started to feel along her abdomen for the long line of sutures. My fingers came up empty as they ran down the smooth, uninterrupted line of her abdomen. In disbelief of what I'd just felt, I had Chrissy lay her on her side. I looked at her abdomen and it was untouched. There was no incision. I took me a second to process what I was seeing.

It was true! The puppies had all been delivered naturally. We had been in such doubt, my mind started to form an apology. For a brief second, I had a feeling of guilt for us branding Anya as a liar. I then started to process the fact that she had let this bulldog deliver naturally. An inherently dangerous and unnecessary risky decision. She didn't even reach out for veterinary advice and call the emergency clinic.

"There were no problems at all during delivery? All ten of these guys came through without an issue? No straining or anything?" I

116

interrogated her, now concerned about the welfare surrounding the delivery.

"Yes. This was no problem. All came out very smoothly on Saturday. No need for vet or surgery. Gucci naturally knows how to do dis. If there was problem, I would call somebody. But I think you will agree, puppies all look very good," she answered confidently back just as I finished Gucci's exam. I knew any lecture I'd give her, would only be a waste of time.

As soon as I stood up, Chrissy saw her cue and immediately got the basket and placed it on the exam table.

It was the first time Anya looked up from her keyboard. She watched me intently as I examined the puppies, eager to make sure they were all healthy. There we six males, and four females. All of them looked great and seemed to be thriving. Chrissy, repetitively announced each one, "How about this one?! Suuurre you don't want a bulldog puppy? They are yourrr favorite breed."

Anya immediately picked up on this. It was the defining moment when her attitude changed toward me forever. I was no longer her lower-level employee, I was now a potential customer. After suggesting X-rays to confirm there were no more puppies, she instantly agreed. There was no need for discussion or provide her with the cost. "If you recommend it, then she needs it! Go take. Take, take, take…" she declared, as if offering us food, rather than consenting to a diagnostic test. Gucci's X-rays were normal and confirmed my initial estimate that there were only ten.

It was a medical miracle to deliver all ten puppies naturally without an issue. Statistically, roughly ten percent of bulldogs are delivered this way. The ten percenters are probably all breeders who possess the same 'expertise' and luck as Anya. Her luck didn't end there. She'd won the bulldog lottery. Having a large litter, and not having to undergo the financial burden of a C-section was a financial win for her. As far as the litter was concerned, unfortunately, some of their luck was about to run out. For one little bulldog, however, his hot streak was far from being over.

Seven-and-a-half Weeks Later

Whether it's a litter of cute puppies or an 'adopt me situation' involving an irresistible pet, I had been down this road with clients before. I'll be the first one to tell you, it's not easy developing this thick armor. But, after years of being put in these predicaments, I have become quite skilled at resisting any temptation to add other pets. I'll casually blow these clients off, and if all else fails I'll use my wife as an excuse. "I wish I could but, my wife will kill me if I bring another [fill in the blank] home." This technique has worked out well for me, and I have avoided falling into the pet-hoarder trap that I have seen a few other colleagues fall into.

I'll confess, being a bulldog lover and having Chrissy bombard me with cute newborn puppies that day, the thought had crossed my mind. The entire day I considered it but as time wore on, I got tired of the idea and had talked myself out it (my skills kicked in). So, by the time the appointment rolled around to give the puppies their first vaccines, I was dead set on blowing off Anya just like everyone else.

Walking into the exam room, Anya was unrecognizable sitting on the bench. She had ditched her goth look and was wearing a long dark-blue flowered dress with sandals. Her hair was back in a ponytail, and she was wearing actual make-up. Her trademark flip phone was nowhere in sight.

Seated next to her was a rather large man who looked to be in his early thirties. His black hair was short, and his bangs were plastered down on his head with gel. He had on black jeans and a black T-shirt with a bedazzled tribal design on it. The T-shirt was a least one size too small and allowed the very bottom of his pot belly to peak out from under every now and then.

On the floor next to them was a massive cage. It contained the typical pandemonium of puppies crying, barking, and playfighting inside of it.

With all the bulldog puppies carrying on, it was difficult to hear Anya great me.

"Good morning, Doctore Miller, this is my cousin Alex."

Alex stood up and shook my hand. Looking up at his large frame, he gave the impression that he could quite easily fill the role of a bouncer or a security guard somewhere.

Without warning, Chrissy, who couldn't contain herself any longer, went over and opened the cage. Instantly the pandemonium spilled from the cage into the exam room. She randomly caught one of the puppies and held it up to me. "This could be your new puppy, Dr. Miller!"

The rest of the puppies bounded out and ran around exploring the exam room. One solitary puppy was left behind. It was in a deep sleep in the corner on the cage and oblivious to everything going on around it.

"Yes! Doctore Miller, Anya says that you are very, very interested in a new puppy," Alex said duplicating Anya's same thick accent. "Let us know which one you want. Two are taken already. They will go very fast, these puppies..." he continued, sitting back down on the bench.

I was listening to the heart on the first puppy. I instantly knew it was normal but, I stalled, continuing to listen, trying to devise the perfect excuse. I decided not to waste any time and employed my go-to: "Yeah, these guys are really awesome. I wish...I wish I could get one. But, you know, the wife. I don't think she'd be down with me getting a bulldog. She's more of a toy breed person."

I figured that would be the end of all the 'Dr. Miller's getting a bulldog' talk. I knew at that moment my popularity with everyone in that room was about to take a big hit. I had been there before and was ready to take the heat.

As I examined the next two bulldogs, everyone was silent. On the third one, Chrissy decided to start her nonsense again. "How about this one?! Suuure you don't want a bulldog puppy?" I was starting to regret letting her in on that appointment. When it came to these types of situations, Chrissy was a sell-out. Jen would have had my back. Chrissy, on the other hand, was always angling to stick me with a new pet.

"Yes, good choice! This one is available, Doctore Miller. I think we have a match, no?"

As I finished the exam on bulldog three, I said, "Yeah, it's a good-looking puppy but... *IF* I was getting one it'd probably be a male. But that's a big *IF*. You know the wife..."

No one actually listened to what I said or they thought I was just joking. The dialog continued, as to which one I wanted. I gave up on bulldog number five, desperately trying to pretend I was focusing on their vaccines and writing up their medical records. It then became a conversation between the three of them. As far as, they were concerned I wasn't even there. They had assigned themselves with picking one out for me.

I caught a break when three bulldogs in a row all turned out to be female. I guess that part they actually heard. When we got to that last bulldog, he was still sleeping in the kennel. Alex had to bend down and reach in to get him.

It was at that moment that Chrissy and I learned, the hard way, that Alex should have either gone with a belt or a larger size of jeans that day. The ones he had on weren't doing him any favors and exposed an area of his backside we'd had been better off not seeing. I think the view even traumatized Chrissy because she didn't start that exam by asking if I was 'suurre' I didn't want a bulldog?

At that point, I thought I might catch a break. Perhaps they had all got the hint and had finally given up. I was moments away from finishing the appointment and dodging another bullet. But Alex interrupted the silence.

"Dis bulldog is my favorite. If you don't want, we may keep. I call him Brutus. But you can change, of course. He is good looking boy, no?"

He was right about that. He was an awesome looking dog.

He had a brown body, white head and neck, and a distinctive brown spot over his right eye. For the first time, the thought crossed my mind, *If* I was going to take one, it would be him. I quickly dismissed the thought. I could sense they were all starting to wear me down. The brainwashing had gone on long enough. It was time to end this appointment. I excused myself and left to go sign their health certificates.

As I started signing them in the treatment area, Chrissy started in again. "You should call your wife, Dr. Miller. You know which one you want. That last dog! It's perfect. That's the one I would choose!"

"That's a great idea!" It was a great idea, but not for the reason Chrissy thought. My wife would put an end to all this. This time it wouldn't be a generic excuse, it would be for real. I'd have an actual phone call to back it all up. I have to admit, I was still under the influence of that really awesome looking bulldog. I was starting to consider it but I knew my wife would help sober me up. She answered on the third ring.

"Hey, honey, it's me. I'm at work and…there is this litter of English bulldog puppies. I'm getting harassed here to get one…so, I said I'd call you and ask. You're not down with us getting one of these dogs, are you?"

"Well… I guess. If you want one. I'd be OK with it…" she replied, sounding more like we were deciding on what to have for dinner, instead of making a lifelong commitment to a dog. I couldn't believe what I was hearing. I was starting to get excited and that wasn't the feeling I was looking for. I knew I had to spell it out for her to make her understand.

"Really? Are you sure? These are *English bulldogs*. As in big drooly dogs. They have many skin and ear problems and that's what makes them kind of smelly. Not to mention all the medical problems...don't get me started on all that. They're not all cute and cuddly. You don't really want one of those? Do you?" I figured that would wake her up. My wife has never been big at multitasking. She was probably focused on something at work. After that speech, I knew she'd come to her senses.

"Yeah, I know, I know. You always focus on all the negative stuff... but what about those puppies?! I bet they are so cute. I think we should get one! But, it's up to you." She had been my last hope at talking me out of what had been brewing for quite some time. Like with all impulse buys, and rash decisions, my adrenaline started to flow.

She had pushed me over the edge and now I was fully on board. All my built-up skills of client resistance had gone right out the window. My obvious answer was yes. I knew exactly who to tell in order to get moral support on this rash decision. I went straight to Chrissy to share the good news.

"Dr. Miller, that's awesome! I'm so excited! I can't wait till everyone hears about—"

"Whoa, maybe we should hold off...um...maybe make it a surprise, like after I pick him up..."

"Uh, OK...I guess. That could be kind of funny...like, catch everyone off guard—"

"Exactly. Don't tell anyone! Especially Jen. Then when I bring him in for the next vaccines, I'll drop the news on everybody then. OK?"

I went back into the exam room and told Anya and Alex the good news. They didn't seem the least bit surprised. I also told them not to tell Liz on the way out, and that I was going to surprise the practice.

I made arrangements with them to pick him up on that weekend. I wanted him to be with Gucci the full eight weeks. Despite what people think, getting kittens or puppies early doesn't make them 'tamer' or better pets. The opposite is true and removing them from Mom too early can result in behavioral problems later on.

Of course, Chrissy wasn't going to keep anything a secret. As soon as I came out of the exam room, Jen nailed me. "What did you go and do now?! Buying an English bulldog puppy? Really, Dr. Miller? Nice. I guess we know who's going to be really taking care of it and treating that dog when its skin and ears get all jacked up. I can't believe Mrs. Miller agreed to that. I hope she knows what she's getting into. It's not going to be cute and cuddly forever...I can't believe you got suckered in like that. So sad, your record is broken for a bulldog."

Deep down I knew she was conflicted. She was happy that I was getting a new dog but at the same time upset that I had fallen victim to the client trap. Furthermore, Jen has done more than her part in adopting cats and dogs. Even though Jen is a far cry from being labeled a veterinary rescue pet snob, she is definitely opposed to purchasing animals.

Nevertheless, ultimately, she came around to the idea and welcomed him with open arms. Like everyone else, she had a new-found affinity for English bulldogs. That didn't stop her from harassing me about it for the next few days.

That Weekend

When I pulled up in front of their house, I had to do a double take on the address. Just like our outside laboratory do when they get a jacked-up lab result; they'll re-run the test and print "verified by repeat analysis" on it. Anya's house address was definitely one you'd want to verify by repeat analysis. I'd already known it was located in a not-so-great neighborhood before I'd embarked on this trip but this street started to remind me of some rough sections in New York City. I made my wife, Kim, wait in the car because I already had the feeling we were at the wrong house. No need to make a production out of it, if we got turned away.

The first time I knocked on the door, I didn't get any response. I started to imagine the lovely resident, and the equally lovely response I'd get from knocking on their door at nine am on a Saturday. I apprehensively knocked on it again. This time, within moments, the door opened and a dude in his early twenties with long hair appeared. He had on boxer shorts, a gray T-shirt, and headphones around his neck.

"Yes?! Can I help you with somethin'?"

"Yeah, I'm here to see Anya?... about a puppy," I responded, already planning on making a quick exit. Just then I heard Anya start yelling at him in her native tongue. I signaled Kim, who made a quick bee-line up the driveway.

The arguing between them continued as he showed us in. Once he made it to the couch, he sat down, put his headphones back on and restarted his video game. Anya continued to yell at him for a good minute even after his headphones were on. Making things even more awkward, she sat us down on the couch right next to him.

"Welcome! You must be excited for new puppy dog. Yes? Let me go get. I show your wife." Anya disappeared to some back room somewhere. Even though she was only gone several minutes, it felt like ages as we sat there awkwardly next to our new gamer friend. I still have no idea who that guy was but I guessed it was her brother. The smell of old cigarette smoke was overpowering. I, however, could swear I smelled something else.

"Hey! You smell that? Smells like..." I leaned over and whispered to Kim making the universal marijuana gesture with my thumb and forefinger as I held them to my lips.

"Shhhhh! He's sitting right next to you. Geez! You think you are whispering but you like never are!" Kim, who did a better job than me, whispered back, making reference to my inherent reputation as a loud talker. It didn't matter anyway because our new young friend was oblivious to anything I said.

Anya eventually reappeared. "Here he is, the beautiful Brutus!" Anya exclaimed as she unceremoniously dumped him in Kim's lap. It was love at first sight. He immediately started licking her and she took to him instantly. Had I been sitting on a couch somewhere else, it might have even looked like a scene out of a Disney movie.

He started to get excited and began crawling back and forth between us. The last time he jumped from my lap up to my face to lick me. It caught me off guard, and I leaned back bumping into the gamer dude seated next to me. He looked at me annoyed and mumbled something in another language. He then went back to his game. I don't know what he said but Anya sure did. She fired back with a line of her own. She then started yelling at him in that same foreign language. He ignored her and continued playing his game as if nothing had happened.

Anya shook her head and motioned us to follow her into her kitchen area. "Come, come. Let's sit and talk. More private. Nice, cozy, and better to talk." She then went on, lowering her voice and whispering, "I not forget. I make special deal for you." I already knew I had reached the business portion of the program and had my checkbook ready in hand.

The discount I was supposedly going to get didn't feel that special when I cut that three-figure check. After writing it, I thought that being one of those adopting veterinary do-gooders sure did seem like the way to go. I also remember the state of her kitchen and it wasn't the nice cozy business-type atmosphere she made it out to be.

Kim and I had already determined his new name on the way over. We both agreed Brutus had to go. Once he sat on Kim's lap in the car, it felt like our choice was the perfect fit. As we got to know him, it

125

seemed even more appropriate later on. We named him Newman, after the (not so) loveable, overweight mail carrier and nemesis to Jerry Seinfeld on the hit TV show *Seinfeld*.

On the drive home, it was apparent that my wife had become overly infatuated with Newman. There was no doubt he was a cute puppy but it took me several months before I was able to figure out her new bizarre affinity for a breed that is an acquired taste.

I have to admit, I was also very excited about having a new bulldog puppy. I tried to dismiss all the thoughts on the congenital medical problems that awaited me later on. Maybe I'd get lucky, and he'd be one of those dogs who have really great genetics. He was AKC registered and maybe that would help swing him in the right direction. Gucci looked pretty good, right?

Well, that all turned out to be a genetic pipe dream. Newman inherited most of the same English bulldog problems as everyone else. He might have got lucky in a few medical departments but he definitely had his fair share of congenital problems. Of course, there was one medical problem he developed that would give me aggravation in both my professional and my home life. I never did completely live that one down, and it is still used against me.

As for Anya and the rest of the litter, they all had a rough start. Anya ended up keeping two female puppies for herself. She told us she was going to partner with Alex in a new business venture breeding English bulldogs. Those two puppies would represent the start of her new "bulldog dynasty."

Unfortunately, they both developed nasty pneumonia. I ended up seeing them again, just a short time after I took Newman home. One puppy did well but the other ended up getting dramatically worse. It was in rough shape when I saw it back for its recheck appointment. I was upset that Anya had let it go on for so long without calling me sooner. It had been off its food for days and could barely breathe. I tried to refer it for critical care at the local specialist and she declined. It was a word I didn't expect or want to hear.

After a lengthy discussion, she started referring to it as a business decision. The appointment quickly went downhill from there. She left telling us she was going to talk to Alex, and then call us back. Of course, that was more of an exit strategy than a real need to discuss anything. Needless to say, she never called back or returned our calls. I never found out what happened to the puppy but my medical prediction for it wasn't good.

The rest of the litter all came to see me, all with individual owners. They all seemed to blend together, and we only saw each of them once. None of them finished the required course of vaccines. All of them also declined heartworm and flea prevention. I never figured out if Anya had phoned them to tell them all to go elsewhere, or they were all the less-than-extraordinary owners Jen had pegged them for. Not a day goes by that I don't wonder about the fate of Newman's brothers and sisters. More importantly, what would have happened to him if he hadn't become a member of our family and his name had been Brutus instead?

Newman's Little Problems

I have always wondered if other medical doctors have the same problems with their immediate family members that I do. Apparently, when I graduated veterinary school my mother and my wife received veterinary degrees alongside mine. I don't know exactly how this works but it seems that they arbitrarily obtained a vast amount of veterinary knowledge when I became a vet. Their knowledge appears to be at least equal to, if not greater, than mine. I have always joked, that my mom is the chief of staff, my wife is the resident, and I'm just the lowly intern. For me, however, the joke isn't always that funny.

Usually, they'll approach me innocently enough with a veterinary question about some extended family member's, or friend's, pet. The person always lives somewhere far, far away so a face-to-face appointment isn't possible. Of course, they also don't want them to bother me with a direct phone conversation. This second-hand way of relaying information would be a lot more convenient for all the parties involved. As an added bonus, it's always some down on their luck situation, which includes a long-winded backstory. Once they get to the actual problem, they're always sure to include a bunch of extraneous information about the pet they think is beneficial, but that only makes the whole ordeal that much more painful.

Eventually, we'll arrive at the crux of the matter, and I'll dispense what I believe to be solid veterinary advice. That's when the real fun begins. Every medical suggestion is questioned and discussed. It's as if I'm back at veterinary school on rounds and being grilled by one of my professors.

After the debate turns into an argument, they'll reluctantly agree with my advice. They'll act like they are only doing so only to appease me. Even though my advice could theoretically work, their more advanced practical ideas are the more currently accepted medical recommendations. Finally, they'll end it by criticizing my argumentative nature, and instruct me that they were only trying to add constructive medical input. If the argument was overly heated, they'll go even further and critique my bedside manner by saying, "I hope you don't talk to your clients like that."

The outcome is always the same, these people fall by the wayside and I rarely receive an actual update. I already know that either my advice worked or they pursued advice elsewhere. Hopefully, in the form of an actual appointment at a vet somewhere. Either way, I learned a long time ago it's best for everyone not to ask and, therefore, avoid another prolonged debate.

However, the situation gets a lot more complicated when it's your own pet, and you can't wait for that anonymous third party to fall off the radar. Diagnosing and treating it also becomes a lot more difficult when you live with a client who thinks they legitimately have a better medical handle on the patient, and the case, than you do. You are now left to discuss the ins and outs of medical conditions on an all-too-frequent basis. That train goes further off the track when there usually isn't actually anything wrong with your pet in the first place. Of course, the one time there actually is something wrong, then you're played out like a sucker. That's exactly how it was with Newman.

Back in those early days, I was still fooling myself into thinking that Newman would be a genetic miracle and not develop any medical issues. I wasn't the only one who was fooling them self. Ever since we'd picked him up, I couldn't understand why my wife, who I thought I knew quite well, had become obsessed with this breed. Soon English bulldog paraphernalia in the form of mugs, calendars, and figurines started to accumulate in our household. Every holiday or birthday greeting card had an English bulldog on it. She would go on to sign Newman's name at the bottom along with everyone else's.

One day looking at them snuggling together on the couch, I finally solved a puzzle that had been nagging at me for a quite some time. My wife had neglected to visualize Newman as an immature form of a dog who would eventually morph into an entirely different adult version. To her, he was a weird-looking variety of cute toy breed dog. She'd looked beyond the inherently obvious bulldog characteristics and latched onto all the traits that made him such a cute and cuddly little puppy. Now, after having raised a bulldog of her own, she will be the first one to warn unsuspecting dog owners that this is one of the ways this breed notoriously suckers you in.

Newman, of course, eventually did grow into that adult version. He grew exponentially in size and developed more adult-bulldog characteristics, such as drooling, farting, and snoring so loudly he had to sleep in another room. The other habit he developed that disheartened my wife, for him it was more like a hobby, was attacking vacuum hoses.

It didn't matter if it was on or off, hidden, or in plain sight. If it was in his zip code he'd find it, and he'd be on a mission to destroy it. Three partially destroyed vacuums later, she was no longer in denial that he was a cute, cuddly weird toy breed.

To say Newman was a unique character or clown would fall short of even remotely describing him. At times he was as equally cunning as

129

his namesake. This made his housebreaking more of a sporting challenge than actual training. It seemed he had a propensity, or took enjoyment, in evacuating his bowels as close to me as possible. He would always accomplish his task without me actually noticing, until, of course, he was long gone. Leaving me alone with his fresh deposit, to exclaim, "Newman!" just as if I was on *Seinfeld.*

Eventually, persistence won out, and he became housebroken. Those types of accidents were then rare occurrences. But, make no mistake, if you had neglected to walk him at just the right time, or rushed back in after a number one, falsely thinking there was no number two, it was game on for Newman.

Newman's other comical behavior was with his toys. When he was younger, he was notorious for destroying his toys in short order. As a veterinarian, I was paranoid enough about having to take him to surgery to remove a toy. Not to mention, the professional embarrassment of having to do surgery on my own dog after preaching to all my clients on what toys they could and couldn't buy. Regardless of how indestructible a toy claimed to be on its packaging, Newman would quickly lay those claims to rest.

My wife, as usual, followed none of my advice. She would throw caution to the wind when it came to purchasing toys for Newman. She'd buy whatever toy she thought 'looked cute' and that Newman 'would really like.' How she knew Newman's actual toy preference, I never did quite figure out. However, I can tell you that if it was a cute plush toy, especially if it had a holiday theme, then according to her, Newman would love it. I would then have to assume the role of the toy police and throw any toy out that looked remotely close to a surgery waiting to happen. Because of this, his toys didn't last long.

As Newman got older, he became less destructive with his toys. They would last longer and it would also open him up to more options. So, little soft Rudolph the Reindeer could potentially make its way into the Easter toy season. After Rudolph lived with Newman long enough, though, he would become a nasty fetid mess of toxic drool. He would be so nasty and unrecognizable, that even Santa's magic washing machine would be unable to rescue poor Rudolph. We would be left with no choice but to lay him to rest. However, this began a new problem and behavior that would further characterize Newman.

No matter how discretely I tried to dispose of the toy, Newman would be instantly aware that it was gone. It didn't matter if he was out for a walk or sleeping in another room. Once he learned it was gone, panic would set in. He would frantically check all the usual locations, and then sit and whine at the place he'd thought it had gone. I, of course, had to learn all that the hard way.

After he witnessed me throw out the first love of his life, a plush, adorable snowman, in our kitchen garbage can, that location became immortalized. It was where he'd go and conduct his infamous sit-in protests if one of his toys suddenly vanished. These protests could go on for days, or even weeks. Sure, he'd take breaks to accomplish his vital daily bulldog chores of sleeping, eating, drooling, and farting but when his scheduled quality play time arrived, he'd be back at the garbage can, sitting, staring, whining, and intermittently letting out a high-pitched bulldog bark that sounded more like a squeal.

This would send my wife on an urgent mission to the pet store to try and hunt down its cute seasonal replacement. Even if she got lucky, and it was the exact same toy, it would take him at least a day to warm up to it. After which, he'd still go to the garbage can, convinced he was missing out on his better toy that was sitting in the garbage. It took us a few years to devise a solution to this problem. We'd buy two, not three, not four, but *two* different toys at the same time. This way he'd still become attached to them both but it would enable them to be replaced in rotation. That would soften but not eliminate the blow, and his sit-ins would be limited to a day or so, instead of weeks.

Newman also went on to develop a routine behavior with his favorite (nasty) toy. He'd take the toy in his mouth while ferociously growling and rubbing it all over you. He didn't really want you to play with him in any kind of logical sense, like fetch or tug of war, he'd just want you to acknowledge his awesomeness and try to take it from him. On occasion, he'd drop it to test you, to see if you had the guts to actually touch it. If you even slightly moved in its direction, he'd ferociously scoop it back up, and celebrate his win by wiping the nasty mess all over you again. Of course, he was only playing. He had the appearance of having the ability to easily take your hand off but he never once bit anyone. It was just his version of a very twisted and gross game.

After my kids were born he'd play a similar game with them. Except, for them, there was no ferocious growling or barking. He'd also drop the toy regularly and let them take it. Unaware of the nasty fate that awaited them, they'd routinely grab it. Then, ever so gently, he'd maneuver his big bulldog head and jowls into position to take it back from them.

To say he was good with kids would fall short of describing just how great he really was with them. English bulldogs are known for being good with children, and Newman excelled in that department. He was more than patient with them and let them do just about anything to him. Anxious to be involved with any activity, or board game they were playing, Newman would notoriously sit in the middle of it, or physically on top of it. It's no coincidence that almost every photo of my children growing up has Newman in it.

We were all having so much fun with Newman his first couple of years, I was still in denial that he'd have any medical issues. Of course, his genetics eventually caught up with him. The two pillars of veterinary dermatology, skin, and ears, were the first to fall. Everyone *thinks* their dog has allergies but, spoiler alert, it's not allergies, it's almost always fleas. In the case of English bulldogs, however, especially here in Florida, then they're usually right. Newman was no exception. In constant need of treatment for his skin or ears, Newman became a regular carpool companion on my commute to work.

I'd be on the speaker phone in the car with my mom. If I'm not on the phone with my practice or my wife, it's usually my mom. I will confess, most of the time I call them, but I do have a forty-five-minute-long commute. Newman's constant panting was always a dead giveaway that he was along for the ride. Assuming her role as chief of staff, she was sure to chime in on my chronic dermatology case. "I hear you have Winston in there with you. What is it? His smelly skin again? You *must* be missing something if it keeps coming back like that. Poor Winston."

My mother hardly ever called him by his actual name, no matter how many times I'd correct her. To her he was Winston. She called him that because there had been a bulldog in my neighborhood in New York City who had been named Winston, after Winston Churchill. It didn't matter that he was long gone, and it had been over thirty years since she'd seen him last. To her he was legendary, and because of that, my bulldog, if not all bulldogs, should be named Winston. It didn't help that my mom had never watched a single episode of *Seinfeld* and had no idea why I'd named him Newman in the first place.

"You mean, Newman. And yes, he has allergies. They cause him to itch, and then his skin gets all infected from him scratching, and that's what smells," I replied, correcting her again.

"It can't just be allergies like you say it is. I think it's gotta be something else. You need to run some more tests. Poor Winston," she'd reply, on a mission to try and get to the bottom of the mysterious skin condition she was convinced he had.

The lowly intern had actually got this one right, and he did, in fact, have allergies. I tried it all; allergy testing, allergy injections, hypoallergenic diets, and even all the latest and greatest allergy medication that veterinary medicine had to offer. None of it worked. If it did work, as Murphy's Law would have it, he'd be the only patient of mine in the entire practice to develop its side effects, like vomiting or diarrhea.

With being on and off medication on a regular basis, Newman developed a real skill or, better yet, an aversion to taking tablets. You could put it or wrap it in any kind of food or treat, and Newman would work it in his mouth like chewing tobacco, find the pill, and spit it out. If you placed it at the back of his throat, he'd partially swallow it, and then regurgitate it out in a frothy foamy mess.

It didn't end there. Any type of treatment, wipe, or bath I tried to give him, he'd disappear to another room, or underneath a table as soon as he saw the bottle. After whatever treatment was done, he'd immediately follow me into the kitchen, to get the treat he felt was well deserved, regardless if the treatment had been accomplished or not.

Even Jen, who is probably the most skilled individual I have ever seen administer medication to a pet, was intimidated by having to medicate him. If he needed medication while he was boarding she'd be sure to tell me about it.

"Sure, Dr. Miller, this all conveniently started now. Right when you are getting ready to go on your little trip. That worked out really well for you, didn't it? Don't worry, we'll treat him, while he's boarding. Of course, we will. I love Newman. Go ahead. Get his treatment plan written up. But don't put him on a bunch of pills that you won't be able to give him yourself after he goes home!"

Of course, his medical issues didn't end with his skin. Like many bulldogs, he definitely had his version of a 'sensitive stomach.' Luckily, he didn't have an actual food allergy but I did have to maintain him on prescription GI diet. There were also only certain things he could eat, and if he ate anything off his pre-approved menu, then all bets were off. After which, we would usually end up in an all-too-familiar situation, with the same hard time from my staff.

"What did he get into this time, Dr. Miller? Nasty! Poor Newman. Let me guess, you want him to board here overnight while *we* take care of the diarrhea. What a shock…"

His special diet helped but didn't eliminate his one iconic bulldog trait, farting. When it came to passing gas, Newman took it to a level of momentous proportions. They were loud, obnoxious, and always

134

comical. Not only were they loud enough to scare even himself, they were one of the few things that could wake him from a deep sleep. After which, he would look around as if something strange had happened to his backside, confused at how his own body could produce such a noise.

Being a bulldog and being notorious for scavenging just about everything and anything, it would become a regular duty for me to pull strands of hair, paper towels, and who knows what else that dangled out of his backside after a number two. Pretty nasty, I know, and you may wonder why I'd share such an intimate detail. Let me explain.

It was a regular occurrence, for my wife and my staff, to page Dr. Miller, STAT, to attend to an emergency backside issue. The most famous of these happened while he was boarding. When the staff brought him to me that time, the "straggler" (as we affectionately referred to these mysterious hangers-on) looked a great deal more complicated than usual.

It had a pink hue to it and was poking in and out of his backside as if it had a mind of its own. It had the appearance of fabric but its elusive nature and location made it hard to ascertain exactly what the object was.

I had just come back from vacation and could not figure out what he could have possibly ingested that would manifest itself almost a week later. He had been boarding in our kennel and had been in our hospital yard under expert supervision. What could this bulldog have possibly eaten now?

Donning a pair of exam gloves, and examining things more closely, I probed around. Grasping hold of it, I gently removed the mysterious item. It wasn't until I held it up that it became recognizable. It was my daughter's tiny pink sock.

How that sock passed through his entire digestive system still remains one of the mysterious, medical miracles of my practice. Make no mistake, pulling anything from your pet's backside is serious business and something that should NOT be done without the guidance of a medical professional. Pulling on a long foreign object could cause a section of bowel to bunch up upon itself like a telescope, making a required surgical case even more complicated. Newman dodged the bullet on having surgery that time but his first major medical issue was just around the corner.

It was just after his fifth birthday and Newman started showing the classic signs of a middle-aged bulldog with arthritis. In the morning, he'd get up and be stiff in his hind legs. It took a while to get going and warm up out of it. Adding arthritis to his list of congenital problems, I started him on a course of anti-inflammatory medication. He improved immediately and, because of this, I continued to procrastinate on putting him under anesthesia to take comprehensive X-rays.

Sometimes, it's like the old proverb about the shoemaker who is so busy, his own children go shoeless. As a solo veterinarian in a busy practice, I can relate to that guy. I was in no rush to start working Newman up, especially when I was convinced he had arthritis. My direct supervisor, my internal-medicine resident (wife), didn't see it that way. She was anxious to get a definitive diagnosis. She wasn't a hundred percent convinced that her intern was right on this one.

Newman did well initially, and he had been off his medication for several months. Coincidentally, it was spring, and starting to warm up in Central Florida so I figured the cold weather had contributed to his arthritis. He was doing so well that even my resident had stopped asking me when I was going to order his X-rays. His signs, however, returned. And when they came back, he developed other more concerning ones.

This time, in addition to being stiff, he had trouble squatting to go to the bathroom, and he was in a lot more pain. He also had the worrying clinical sign of leaving little turds in his bed (fecal incontinence). I didn't need my resident to tell me something more serious was going on. The procrastinating was over. I took X-rays of both his hips and his back. They confirmed he had arthritis in his hips but they also suggested another more serious problem. It was one that I wouldn't be able to treat.

I had to take him to our local specialist to confirm it. After she read his MRI, the neurologist confirmed Newman had lumbar-sacral stenosis. In Newman's case, there was instability in the vertebrae at the level of his pelvis. This instability led to a chronic change in his disk that caused it to compress his spinal cord. The treatment was surgery. I did get a professional discount on that one but it was still a costly surgery.

It required the second three-figure check I cut for Newman. Like the first, it was worth every penny. Newman did great and, unlike a person going through back surgery, was back to normal in just a few days. It was more of an issue keeping him calm and quiet for two weeks after his surgery. Of course, Jen completely understood and didn't complain when I decided on boarding him for that crucial period of strict kennel rest and medication administration.

For the record, the orthopedic specialist also looked at Newman and confirmed he had arthritis in his hips. The specialists will be the first to tell you lumbar-sacral stenosis can be a hard condition to diagnose. Because older dogs are more commonly affected, they typically already exhibit signs of arthritis that affect their hind end function. This can lead to a lot of overlap between the two conditions, not to mention that earlier, milder cases can respond to anti-inflammatory medication. Just like in Newman's case.

To my wife, all that didn't matter. I had missed the diagnosis on her baby, all because I didn't listen, and I was too lazy to work him up. From that time on, she was all in my business, trying to directly supervise every little medical issue Newman had. It didn't matter that she forgot the name of the particular condition he had. All she needed to say was, "I was right that time you missed that *thing* with this back. You didn't listen, and I was right!" Regardless if he was actually sick or not, I was already behind the eight ball with anything else I tried to explain.

Fortunately, he remained fairly healthy for a while after that particular episode. He had a few imagined illnesses but, as far as the real medical history, it was pretty straightforward. Kim and my mom would still tend to exaggerate everything. The prime example of this was the time my daughter left her BBQ chips on the coffee table.

Newman made short work of those and had some really nasty diarrhea. I had to hospitalize him on fluids, and it lasted for several days. Of course, just to be safe, I boarded him for close to a week. It was worth hearing Jen complain that time, in order to ensure my house would be spared from any future blowouts.

I had seen it all before and tried to reassure Kim. She wasn't convinced. She thought Newman had a real risk of actually dying. Then, when it took a couple days for his diarrhea to resolve, she was quick to throw out my diagnosis of 'dietary indiscretion,' and start adding things like cancer, and liver failure to the list. My mom got in the mix when she heard he was still hospitalized. "Peter, I used to give the dogs all kinds of things, they never had diarrhea, ever. I never had to take them to the vet for those kinds of things. Not to mention keep them at the vet office for days like that. He's still there with diarrhea? Something is wrong with him, Peter. I think you need to do some more tests and find out what it is. Poor Winston."

When he finally did go back home, I got the impression from both of them that I should have fixed things a lot sooner. If it was just diarrhea how could it take that long to fix? They were still convinced that I must have missed something. They said they knew it would come back, and it was just a matter of time. When it did come back, they said, I would then run the *right* test and find the answer. Of course, they didn't specifically tell me what *that test* was exactly. It never returned like they predicted. It didn't stop them from trying to tie every soft or loose stool for months or even years later back to that particular episode.

As Newman became a senior citizen, his little medical issues would become more frequent. In typical fashion, they'd be blown out of proportion and my medical knowledge would be questioned on a more regular basis. After he had just turned ten, however, it reached a new level.

Monday 5:32 PM

MILLER, NEWMAN Age: 10 Yrs.

It never failed. When something was wrong with Newman, Kim would wait until my drive home to drop the bomb on me about something.

"He just threw up! Again. It was his entire dinner. It's his food and a bunch of foam and drool. It's so disgusting, thank goodness it's on the tile—"

"NASTY! I'm going to puke!" I could hear my daughter yell out in the background.

"Again? He threw up before?" I asked, trying to get a history, on my own dog.

"Well, yeah. It was only bile this afternoon, he always does that every so often so I wasn't too worried."

"What's he like? Is he lethargic or…"

"He sleeps all day. It's hard to tell. He is usually more excited when the kids get home but today he seemed more, more subdued… Oh yeah! did you bring his food home? Like I asked?"

"No, I forgot. You should have called me to remind me about the food. Then you could have told me about the vomiting," I replied.

"He just vomited. What would you have done anyway? I did tell you about the food, you just don't remember. You need to take him in tomorrow. Run some tests, there is something wrong with him…"

She had me there about the food. She was also right, I probably wouldn't have taken any medication home, or had her bring him in anyway. But anytime anything was wrong with Newman her solution was always the same: "Take him in. Run some tests." I was already not planning to take him in or run any of those tests. I had my own test for him when I arrived home.

When I walked in, Newman was waiting for me. He got all excited when I came through the door. He did his best as a geriatric dog with arthritis to try and jump up on me. Just like I suspected, that test was completely normal. That wasn't the only thing waiting for me.

I could see his large pile of foam and vomit on the tile floor in the kitchen.

"Hurry, Dad! Clean that stuff up before I puke. I'm getting sick just looking at it!" my son immediately chimed in.

Yeah, that's right, Dr. Miller is permanently assigned that procedure. Now, before you go jumping to any conclusions, I'll be the first one to tell you when it comes to any type of messy situations, my wife is a rock star. She's a mom, and she can deal with all sorts of nasty business with the best of them; situations with our kids that would turn my medically trained stomach. If he'd only produced bile, she'd have been OK. But when it came to full-on, nasty bulldog stomach contents, that was a procedure she wasn't qualified to handle. Those types of specialty cases she referred to Dr. Miller.

The next morning, I fed Newman only half of his normal meal. I wanted to give his stomach a chance to rest and, truth be told, that was all that was left of his special food. As per usual, he inhaled it. He wasn't looking or acting sick to me. So, against my resident's instructions, I left him at home. When I got to work, I went straight to the back of the hospital to grab Newman's food and load it into my car. There was no way I was going to forget it this time.

On the way home that night, Kim had reported that Newman was back to normal. She made sure to remind me that he was half-starved and out of food. She didn't concur on feeding him half his normal meal that morning. It was against her better medical judgment, and it was her view that I had deprived him only because of my forgetfulness.

There is no doubt about it, my resident is tough, and I didn't get any credit for remembering his food this time, or making the right call on not bringing him in. In her mind, she was convinced she was right about those tests. The only reason she didn't chew me out that time was out of the kindness of her own heart.

Wednesday 5:34 pm

"Newman was kind of…I don't know…just blah today. He only ate a few bites of his dinner. I'm worried something is wrong." Unlike some other breeds, when it comes to bulldogs, it's either 'inhale my food' or 'I'm sick.' Kim was right to be concerned. That is if she wasn't exaggerating again.

"Did he eat his breakfast OK? Any vomiting? Any diarrhea? Anything else going on?" I asked her in rapid-fire succession, already worried, and frustrated that something may actually be wrong with him.

"Yeah, he ate it but like …not at his normal pace. I knew you should have taken him in and run those tests."

I used the same test as I did on Monday night. When I walked through the door he went ballistic with excitement. He followed me into the kitchen, went right over to his food and inhaled it. After which, he drank a large amount of water. As he ran to get his toy, he trailed slobber all over the kitchen floor, which I would end up slipping in later on. He then promptly rubbed the fetid mess of drool that used to resemble a plush Uncle Sam, all over my dress pants.

"Looks pretty normal to me," I triumphantly declared.

"Normal, huh? Then why was he all lethargic today? How come he waits for you to get home to eat and only then perks up? You know he's not a hundred percent. What do you think is going on?" she asked as if she knew the answer and was only quizzing me. Waiting to see if I got it right.

141

"You know these freaking kids, man, they probably left something lying around. Who knows what he found and ate. He probably had a mild bout of pancreatitis that caused the vomiting, and him being lethargic the last few days," I confidently responded. That was as good a diagnosis as any. The resident wasn't going to trip me up this time. She knew I was most likely right but, of course, had to one-up her intern and make me work.

"I don't think so. I don't think it's table food, you always say that. I'm really good about cleaning everything up. I don't think he got into anything. They're older now. They aren't toddlers anymore. It's not like they drop stuff all over the floor. I still think something is wrong. You need to take him in tomorrow and run some tests."

It was the same excuse I hear all the time at work and at home. It's always table food until proven otherwise. Even in my own house, I can't trust these people. Newman is resourceful, and with my kids, who knows what he could have stolen from whatever they left lying around. I was convinced of my diagnosis.

Without any major signs, vomiting, or diarrhea he'd be fine. This is why, against her direct orders, I left Newman home again the next day. He continued acting like his old self on Thursday. I knew time would go on to prove me right on this one. That would keep my resident out of my hair for a while. That is until Friday rolled around.

Friday 12 pm

We had just finished our last appointment, and we were all getting ready to go to lunch. Just then Liz came on the treatment area speakerphone: <BEEP!> "Dr. Miller, it's Kim on line one."

My wife never, ever calls me at work. There are times that I get into arguments with her because I feel she should have called me for something important and she didn't. Her answer is always the same, saying she didn't want to bother me at work. Downplaying whatever it was and saying it could have waited.

"What's the matter?" I asked, my mind racing that something serious had happened.

"I tried to text you and call your cell phone but you didn't answer. Newman didn't eat his breakfast. He's been lethargic all morning. I don't care what you say. I'm on the way with him. You're running blood work, doing X-rays, or whatever! He's sick, and you need to figure out what's wrong with him."

12:30 pm

As soon as Kim came into the treatment area, Newman was all excited to see Jen and Cassey. Jen had been out of the loop on this one until Kim told me she was on the way. I was then obligated to come clean, on the case. Even though I pay her salary, and she is considered my head technician, when the case involves my resident, Jen is pretty much in agreement with Kim on just about everything.

My resident has a different way of actually working up her cases, and it begins with Jen. Kim will quite freely discuss things and bounce ideas off Jen. Jen, in return, will have no problem with voicing her own medical opinions, all of which Kim will regard highly, and wholeheartedly agree with. Armed with this new perspective and knowledge from Jen, Kim will then end up discussing all these insights at length with me for days on end.

"Don't worry, Mrs. Miller, we'll have his blood work and X-rays done in just a little bit." And yes, in case you were wondering, the resident gets all her tests done without any back talk. Jen and she for some reason also have a more professional working relationship.

Jen handed the blood work to Kim and proudly informed her everything was normal. They had me read the X-rays of chest and abdomen for them. After I determined they were all normal, Jen and Kim both nodded in agreement, as if they were testing me. When I recommend a urinalysis, and the blood test to check his pancreas, Kim reluctantly agreed. She reminded me she was certain he didn't get any table food, and the pancreas test was a waste of time.

143

They both thought the urinalysis was a good idea and as soon as I mentioned it, Jen even stated to Kim, "It's never a bad idea to have a look his urine just to be thorough." She then went on to say, "Don't worry about Newman, we'll keep an eye on him this afternoon. I'll offer him a canned version of his food to see if I can entice him to eat. Dr. Miller can take him home tonight, no problem. Don't worry. If anything changes, we'll call you. I think he's going to be fine. Probably just an upset stomach or something like that."

And with a quick peck on the cheek for me, my resident left. But the version of Jen that I knew, instantly returned.

"You're welcome, Dr. Miller. You're lucky that work up was for Mrs. Miller and Newman, or you'd definitely be owing us lunch or something. In fact, you should still get us lunch this week. You should have brought him in this morning. Oh yeah, Mrs. Miller told me all about how she's been *begging* you to bring him in. You make your poor wife drive all the way out here, and we miss our regular lunch. All because you're too lazy to bring him in. Now I have to cram my lunch down my throat in the next twenty minutes before the appointment gets here. Nice! You owe us."

I never did get her the lunch she was looking for, at least not for that.

That weekend, my resident continued to grill me looking for a diagnosis. My answer was always the same, he ate something he shouldn't have. She was trying to trip me up again but it didn't work. When Newman was acting completely normal over the entire weekend, I had proved to her I was right. At least I thought I had proved it.

His pancreas test and urinalysis both came back completely normal on Monday. And Monday night, when he didn't eat his dinner, Kim had all the evidence she needed to drop this case back in my lap. I may be just the intern to these people but I knew exactly how to get a definitive diagnosis on this case. I knew who would give me the exact answer I was looking for, and finally get my resident off my back once

144

and for all. That week I scheduled an abdominal ultrasound with Dr. Maria DeSantis.

Dr. DeSantis was a specialist in internal medicine. Instead of working at a specialist hospital, she had a mobile practice. She traveled to general practices with all her ultrasound and other equipment in her SUV. I had been using her services at my practice for over ten years. She had gone to Cornell and done her residency at Animal Medical Center in New York City, two meccas of veterinary medicine. She was brilliant and well-respected among other specialists.

She was five two, thin, and she wore thick-rimmed black glasses. Her black hair was always in a ponytail. She was originally from Brooklyn, and her comebacks were fast and witty. Those who didn't know her might stereotype her as a nerd, but we knew her better than that. My staff adored her. They enjoyed her sense of humor, and whenever she was scheduled, it was a like an event they all looked forward to.

Later that Week

My mother could hear Newman panting in the car on the ride to work that day. Had I been smart, I would have come up with a cover story like his skin but I couldn't lie to my own mother. I had to explain the whole entire case to her. Not surprisingly, she became bored halfway through and stopped paying attention to what I was saying. Apparently, this case was too boring for her to offer her medical opinion. So, as chief of staff, she decided to take a more supportive role instead. She interrupted me toward the end and started talking over me.

"—Poor Winston. I think you're making a smart decision. Good thing you have that nice lady to check your work for you."

"She's not checking *my work*. It's a second opinion by an internal-medicine specialist. Like, you know, when human doctors refer a case to another specialist doctor. I'm like the family doctor, and she's a specialist. She'll do an ultrasound, and then will give me a second opinion."

"I know! That's why I said it's a good thing you have that specialist lady go over your work for you. It's never a bad idea to have someone check over your work. You probably missed something. Maybe because it's your own dog or what have you. I hope she finds out what's wrong with poor Winston."

I was starting to think that maybe I had missed something. I was glad his ultrasound appointment was in the morning because now I was starting to get anxious about Newman.

When Jen brought Newman into the exam room where Dr. DeSantis had set her gear up, Newman pushed the exam-room door open. He ran to the end of his leash and tried to jump up on her leg.

"He doesn't look too sick to me, Dr. Miller. You sure those kids of yours didn't slip him somethin'?" Dr. DeSantis replied, as she bent down and rubbed Newman's head. Her New York accent, like mine, had been dialed down from living outside of New York for so long. But it was still recognizable.

She bent down and started to examine Newman. It took all her reflexes to avoid being licked by him. I had planned on being there the whole time and being able to get the play by play. It had now become a puzzle, which I wanted to verify I had solved correctly. To say I had a point to prove would have been an understatement. She had just finished his exam and was looking at his X-rays when Cassey appeared next to me.

"Hey, Dr. Miller, your next one is here."

"Next one? I thought the next one wasn't for another half-hour?" I asked venting my frustration at her and upset I was going to have to wait even longer to get my answer.

"What do you expect me to do, Dr. Miller, we just got a walk-in. It's to check ears. Itching last few days. We are a veterinary practice, people do bring in sick animals," she sarcastically replied. It seems the more years that she worked with Jen, the braver she's become. I knew it would be only a matter of time before I was completely outnumbered by them.

"See ya, Dr. Miller. It's probably better that way so Dr. DeSantis can get her work done without you asking a bunch of questions. Besides, our conversations are way more interesting when you're not here. Right, Dr. DeSantis?" Jen quipped.

"I'm not getting in the middle of you two again. I learned that a long time ago. You two are like an old married couple. You're on your own on that one, Jen," Dr. DeSantis replied, now holding Newman's lab work in her hand.

"Dr. DeSantis is just being professional and doesn't want to hurt your feelings. Me, I'll tell it to you like it is, Dr. Miller. Just go do your appointment. By the time you're done with that, she'll be all finished here. No problem," Jen replied legitimately attempting to console me for missing out on my own pet's exam.

"You sound pretty confident about that, Jen. I didn't know I had a fan club," Dr. DeSantis chimed in.

"You do and I'm definitely one of your fans. That's why I keep telling you, you need to hire me. I can be like your permanent tech. Instead of dealing with all those riff-raff techs you probably get at all those other practices, you'd have me. I'd be a trip. I could definitely keep you entertained. Then, I'd get to ride around with you all day, instead of being stuck in here—"

"I know who'd get the short end of that deal. Trust me. Once the honeymoon is over, it's all downhill. Ask me how I know," I replied interrupting Jen.

"Be quiet, Dr. Miller! You're just jealous. Keep it up, and you'll lose me to the highest bidder one day…watch!" Jen fired back.

"Uh-oh, Dr. Miller, you don't want to lose Jen. Good thing for you both, I'm not bidding. You better get going. Don't worry, we'll take care of your baby," Dr. DeSantis said, trying to mediate, as she drew

147

up Newman's sedation in a syringe. Some pets are perfectly comfortable lying on their backs for an ultrasound but we knew well in advance that Newman wasn't one of those.

Cassey handed me both the record and the otoscope in an effort to move me on to the appointment. I looked over the record and it was a name I didn't immediately recognize: Nicholson, Danny Boy. I was hoping for a simple ear infection, so I could get back to Newman's ultrasound, and Dr. DeSantis. As a rule, socializing with other veterinarians is something I usually try to avoid at all costs. But I really like Dr. DeSantis. She's cool and definitely an exception to that rule.

I had planned on getting things over in a hurry but when I went into the exam room my hopes were crushed. The *emergency* walk-in ear infection turned into emergency vaccinations, along with an emergency nail trim. Usually, I pawn off doing any nail trims. It's one perk of being the doctor, that even Jen can't dispute. Once in a while, I'll step up to the plate and do the staff a solid. I will admit, it is not a common occurrence, and I always stack the deck by choosing a pet that's really well-behaved. Regardless, I never let the opportunity go to waste, and I'll remind them what a good boss they have.

This, however, was an Australian shepherd. Despite being a perfect angel for the entire appointment, Danny Boy wanted no part of the nail trim. It took all of Cassey's skills to hold him. It was one of those nail trims that make me look like a complete amateur in front of the owners. After I got the last nail clipped, I thought that I could finally make my exit. I was going to hand the appointment over to Cassey for her to wrap it up and to go over the ear meds. Instead, I was bombarded by a bunch of questions by both his owners. As I was answering them, I could hear the murmured laughing of Jen and Dr. DeSantis through the exam room wall. It sounded like a really good time and I was missing out on it.

When I finally came out of the exam room, it was like a party but with all the excitement over. I had arrived too late. Jen and Newman were both gone, and Dr. DeSantis was alone in the exam room typing on her laptop. The lights in the exam room were now back on and the ultrasound was over. She had even put all her ultrasound equipment back in her car. I leaned in through the open exam-room door.

"Everything OK? No bad news... I hope..." I reluctantly asked.

"Nah, not at all, Dr. Miller. Old Newman, he's fine. I agree with you, he probably ate something he shouldn't have. Since his vomiting has stopped, I'd continue the arthritis meds like you've already been doing. I grabbed a urine from him, and you'll need to send it in to the lab for a culture. If the culture is negative (normal) and he's still not eating, call me. I do want you to start him on Prilosec in case he's got some GI ulceration going on. I also think we keep him on the canned diet for a week. Jen tells me he seems to be inhaling that, so maybe we'll get a better idea of his appetite on it. Here's the written version...." Just as she finished her summary, she grabbed the report from her printer and handed it to me.

After an abdominal ultrasound, Dr. DeSantis routinely orders urine culture to be thorough. They almost always come back negative. I wasn't too worried about that. More importantly, she said, 'Newman is going to be fine.' Finally, someone was on my side. And this wasn't just anyone, this was a boarded specialist. This was just the case I needed to put me back on top. 'That thing with his back' would be long-forgotten. Now, I would have my own thing to use. "Remember the time you ordered that unnecessary ultrasound? Remember when I told you he got into something?"

I fully expected Newman to be completely back to normal. It was the main reason why, when it came to talking trash to my wife, I wasted no time in getting an early start. I even brought home a copy of Dr. DeSantis' report to show her. I unabashedly harassed my resident. Every time he inhaled his food or brought me his fetid toy to play with I'd say, "Real sick. Maybe we need to run another test, like an MRI." I didn't know it then but, while I thought I was celebrating another medical victory, I was actually digging my own grave.

149

Three days later, he refused to even eat the canned food at dinner time. Now, the tables had turned, and my resident was more than ready to hold me accountable. In a sick twist of medical irony, she started to use my own words against me.

"Maybe he needs to go back to the neurologist and have an MRI. He might have another one of those *things* with his back again."

I knew it wasn't his back but I was at a loss for an explanation. I was starting to seriously worry about Newman all over again. The only plan I had was to wait for his culture results to return. I wasn't looking for an actual result this time. Instead, I was only regarding it as a formality. More importantly, I knew I'd be able to get Dr. DeSantis' opinion after it came back.

8:33 am

As soon as I arrived, I immediately proceeded to the box of records with my pending lab work. I dug out 'Miller, Newman' from the pile. Before I even opened his record, Jen, as always, clued me in that she'd already looked at his results.

My staff are always entitled to look at results and, obviously, they have no choice but to see them when they collate them for the patient's record. However, whenever they see results before me, it feels like an invasion of privacy. It's like they've opened my mail and read it. It felt worse because not only was it my own dog, the person delivering the news was Jen. Of course, there was more.

"Looks like Mrs. Miller was right about that ultrasound. I can't wait till she finds out she made the right call on that. Poor Newman. I'm glad we finally found out what was wrong with him..."

I decided to ignore her. There was no comeback for this one. It might have been my decision to order the ultrasound but I had hung this test on my resident. Instead of it being used to mark her downfall, it was hers to take all the credit on. I pretended to be preoccupied with writing the results in Newman's record.

150

Despite my silence, Jen continued, "Dr. DeSantis is good. Real good. Now you know why she does all these cultures. I had a feeling he had an occult UTI. It all makes perfect sense." Whenever a test comes back, Jen is quick to get on the bandwagon one way or another. Regardless of the test results, she always has a premonition and (you guessed it) it's never wrong.

I figured I could shield myself, at least temporarily, by calling Dr. DeSantis. Jen realized I was ignoring her and turned her attention to Cassey to gloat even further. As if by miracle, Dr. DeSantis answered on the second ring and rescued me.

"Oh hey, Dr. Miller. I'm thinking you got those culture results back. Wait! Let me guess he's got a UTI."

"Yeah, he's got a UTI. I hope this is the answer to all my problems because he didn't eat last night, or this morning," I replied sheepishly, after which I went on to dictate his complete results to her.

"Now you know why I always do all those cultures. I'd start him on *Orbax*. I'd do another culture, in a month. If he doesn't improve in the next few days, or you have any questions, call me. Don't forget to fax me a copy of his culture. And OH yeah! Good luck with your resident and all that. Later, Dr. Miller!"

As she hung up, I heard her let out a laugh. I immediately confronted Jen, "You didn't tell, Dr. DeSantis my joke about my wife being the resident and all that, did you?!" I asked without even making an attempt to hide my anger.

"Calm down, Dr. Miller. Dr. DeSantis is like family. It's almost like she works here. She gets it. She thought it was hilarious. You're too sensitive. It's not like you specifically told me *not to* tell her. Did you? Let us know what antibiotics to get up for Newman. At least you know he's going to be OK. Aren't you at least happy about that?" she said patronizing me in an effort to calm me down.

She had a point, I never specifically told her not to say anything. But we know she would have told her all that anyway. I belted out Newman's Orbax (antibiotic) dose. I then thrust the record in front of her, so she could read it as she filled his script.

I then grabbed the phone to call my wife to explain it all to her. I knew she was worried. Flipping between the normal vet script I use on my clients and talking as a husband is always awkward for me. No matter what, it seems I can never balance conveying the information in a professional yet personal manner. I explained to her, again, that a urinalysis can be completely normal, and a patient can still have a UTI. An occult UTI is one that is only detected when the urine is actually cultured to check for bacterial growth.

"See, see. I was right. Wasn't I? I'm so relieved! I really thought something serious was wrong with him. Hopefully, this finally works. I'll be happy when he's all back to normal. That poor baby." It was clear my resident was trying to be nice and take the high road. Only time would tell if she was really that nice and understanding or just using that to further demonstrate her superiority over me.

Eventually, my chief of staff circled back around and checked in with me. "How is old Winston doing with everything?" I broke down and gave her the lengthy explanation. I rehashed the last part of the case in detail. She talked over me again as I got toward the end, and said, "I knew that doctor from Brooklyn would help you. She's one smart cookie!"

They never did understand all that occult UTI stuff. To them, I'd somehow missed the obvious UTI on the urinalysis I did and, thankfully, I had enough brains to get someone to review my sloppy work. Instead of this case putting me back on top, it put me even further down the veterinary hierarchy. It became known as '*that* urine sample I didn't read properly,' and it was yet another case they would continue to use against me.

Newman made a complete recovery over that next week. He didn't have any medical problems, at least any major ones, after that little episode. I thought he was on track to fulfill our hopes and aspirations of shattering the record for life expectancy. The average life expectancy for an English bulldog is eight to ten years of age. I've heard legends of bulldogs living for sixteen years but the oldest one I have ever seen was fourteen and that was my goal for Newman.

Three months before his twelfth birthday, I had to make one of the most painful decisions of my career. It's always been easier helping clients make that decision but now it was with Newman. He'd started getting senility issues when he'd turned eleven and they had got a lot worse. His arthritis was barely under control with his medication and it had become increasingly more difficult to give it to him. With a pile of normal diagnostic tests, it was apparent that his body was giving out due to age. There was no specialist or treatment I could summon to fix him.

When his bad days were overwhelmingly outnumbering the good ones, we knew it was time. It was then that we made one final decision. I put Newman to sleep. We were all devastated. I did my part in hiding it, especially on that day, but it took me a long time to get over it. He left a void that will be difficult to fill. I still miss Newman and as far as I'm concerned there will never be another bulldog like him.

I always wondered, when his time came, would I be like many of my own clients and elect to keep Newman's ashes? I have always completely understood my clients' decisions but actually doing it myself made me feel uneasy. Part of this may lie in the fact that my mother had all our poodles cremated and rather than have them out in plain sight, she chose to keep the urns in undisclosed locations hidden around the apartment.

I can remember being startled by finding an urn in the living room corner behind the vertical blinds. Startled, I confronted my mom and asked why she had chosen that location. She confessed that she'd forgotten whose urn it actually was but was confident she'd placed it there because they liked to sun themselves in the living room. It didn't matter that the urn was stuck on the floor in the corner, deprived completely of any sunlight. To her, it was a perfect location.

When I put Newman to sleep, my mom was equally devastated. As a dog owner who had been there, and consummate dog lover, she completely empathized. In addition, for reasons I can't explain, she never mistakenly referred to him as Winston again. For her, it wasn't a question of *if* Newman was going to be cremated, it was only a question of where I was going to put his ashes. After I lost Newman, I decided that I needed a family vacation, and picked the Bahamas as the destination. Upon hearing that, my mom said she had the perfect idea.

She suggested I bring Newman along with us and scatter his ashes on the beach. I completely vetoed that idea. I explained to her, how I'd probably end up having some customs agent, or their trained sniffer dog stumble upon poor Newman. Then, I'd be forced to explain, he wasn't any kind of illicit substance. I'd be left to try and prove my now awkward, innocent situation to them in front of an audience full of tourists.

That didn't stop my mom from doing the legwork on what she thought was a great idea. The next day, she went to a local vet's office a block from her apartment building. I can only imagine the conversation that took place. Some poor receptionist at the desk was forced to hear my entire life story, including that I was a veterinarian myself and that I had recently put my beloved English bulldog to sleep. I can only imagine what that practice thought of my mom's story. If that vet ever decides to write a book, though, you're welcome!

That night she called me with great excitement and declared, "The nice young girl went back to the vet, and asked, and everything. They said it's completely legal and official and what have you. You can take Newman to the Bahamas!"

Newman never did make it to the Bahamas. However, I did get his ashes returned. When the time came, the decision was obvious. On our mantle, over the fireplace, there sits a cedar box. On top of that box, is an English bulldog figurine donated from my wife's collection. It stands proudly on top, guarding a gold nameplate that says "Newman."

Newman Miller, eleventh birthday celebration

Old Man and the Millennials

When you've been working in the same practice for as long as I have, you start to notice things. You see pets grow old before your eyes. Their records get thick, and it feels like just last year they were a family's latest addition. Now, they are geriatric versions of their former selves and have a laundry list of medical issues that you have to contend with to keep them going. It seems clients and their families seem to age at a pace equal to their pets. Kids that could barely look over the exam table are now going to college and their parents are now elderly.

Of course, that was all fun and games when I had been the young vet. Back then, I could look at all these people as if I would always remain my youthful self. I was in denial, thinking I'd never really age, at least not like them. I'd still always be the cool vet. That all goes out the window when those clients' kids grow up, and they still always call you, sir. All those cool jokes and movie references you once had, now fall flat in the exam room. You start feeling like an old comic from another generation who's lost his edge.

Nothing highlighted this fact more than when Melissa returned. Melissa was one of those on-and-off-again employees. Jen was always conflicted about her employment. Jen complained to me about her when we had her and missed her when she was gone. When she left us the last time, it was to pursue a nursing degree, and we all thought that time it was for good.

We saw Melissa again when she adopted a female chihuahua named Frankie, and it was in need of vaccines. We found out on that visit, that she had dropped out of nursing school. She said she quickly realized that nursing wasn't for her and she missed working with animals. Jen who always feels overworked welcomed the opportunity to potentially get some much-needed relief. Jen managed to con us both that day, and I hired her back.

Melissa was the youngest employee in our practice. I never used to get hung up on the whole generational thing, including all the cute nicknames for each generation. However, Melissa was in the generation after Jen and me, and the cultural differences were obvious. Every song, TV show, movie, or celebrity we'd bring up, Melissa would have no idea what the hell we were talking about. At times it felt like Melissa was from an entirely different country, let alone another generation.

Despite all her generational differences, we all welcomed her back with open arms. As usual, it was as if she had never left. Jen was quick to point out that Melissa needed a welcome-back party. I tried to blow the suggestion off, especially when Jen told me its location. Jen wanted to hold it at Liz's favorite Sunday brunch spot, famous for its hamburgers, Bloody Marys, and flamboyant singing divas. I thought I'd be able the squash that idea by stalling and telling them I was thinking about it. It was of no use. They were all hell-bent on going, with or without me.

As much as I appreciate my staff, I know it's a lot more fun when the boss isn't around. Not to mention, getting singled out and serenaded by a diva, at the amusement of my slightly buzzed staff is not my idea of a relaxing Sunday. So, as usual, I used my family as the perfect excuse to bow out of that 'girl's day out.' I may not officially have attended that party but my practice credit card sure did. It apparently had a spectacular time. It seems like no expense was spared to ensure that Melissa (Jen) had the welcome-back party she deserved.

Monday 8:32 am

On Monday, I heard all the details about their little party and it only further supported my decision to bail on that brunch. There was a silver lining in it for me. Apparently, it was the perfect team-building exercise they all needed to put them all in a good mood, especially Jen. That became more apparent when Jen handed me the record for Solie Martel.

"I know who it is, and it's Monday but, please, try and stay in a good mood, sir. Don't bring us all down on this one. Come on, it will be fine."

The Martels were snowbirds from Quebec. Even though our practice is far removed from the more popular snowbird destinations like the beaches of South Florida, we still get more than our fair share of them. When the hometown veterinarian has a unique way of practicing, it can sometimes make dealing with patients an ongoing ping-pong match over differing medical opinions. Add in a difficult client, and it makes the situation worse. This is why every spring, when practices up north ask for certain records, Jen will proudly announce, "It's so and so's problem now. Enjoy that one!" as she faxes the offending record across. Of course, the celebration is short-lived as they inevitably return six months later.

As far as Solie (soul-ee) Martel is concerned, despite being a cute little Maltese, with an equally cute name, she was an insanely difficult patient to deal with. A lot of this can be attributed to her ongoing anxiety issues. But that was nothing compared to dealing with Mrs. Martel.

Truth be told, Jen's pep talk started to have an effect on me. I was comforted by her good mood, and that she'd be going in the exam room right there with me. Jen excels at holding difficult patients and having her in the room to deal with Mrs. Martel is an added bonus. Jen knows both what to say, and when to say it in order to keep Mrs. Martel calm. I also always feel better when I have someone in the room who I know shares my opinion on the situation.

As far as the Martels are, or more specifically Mrs. Martel is, concerned, Jen and I are on the exact same page. Just as I started to feel a bit of relief, Jen handed the record to Melissa.

"Here you go. This will be the perfect appointment to get back into the groove." Jen, immediately sensing my disappointment, tried to comfort me again. "Don't worry, Dr. Miller, Melissa is a pro. You'll be fine. Trust me."

159

All the relief I felt was immediately replaced by anxiety. Melissa was no Jen, and the Martels aren't anyone's ideal first appointment. I was in no position to try to argue and get Jen back in the mix. It would only show Melissa that we had no confidence in her abilities, and regardless, Jen was not going to switch with her. As far as Jen was concerned, she had a new get-out-of-the-exam-room free card and its name was Melissa. I tried to stay positive.

My positive attitude immediately vanished when I entered the exam room. Mrs. Martel was sitting on the exam-room bench with her head between her legs. In addition, the other exam-room door had been left open for her. She had informed us at her very first appointment that she suffered from claustrophobia and requested we leave it open until the actual appointment started.

"You can close that door now if you want to," Mr. Martel commanded in a thick French accent, as he sat on the bench rubbing Mrs. Martel's back. He was wearing black pants, a button-down, short-sleeve red plaid shirt, and black sneakers. His hair was gray and parted to the side, but his thick mustache was jet black. It stood out compared to his gray hair, and I always suspected it was dyed. It was so out of place that it always made it difficult to talk to him without staring at it. Mrs. Martel was wearing a white T-shirt, jeans, and sandals. Her head was buried between her legs and all I could see was the top of her curly gray hair.

"Yeah, I'll close that so we have a little more privacy." I've never been a proponent of broadcasting my exam-room dialog into the waiting area. "How's Solie been doing?" I asked, hoping for a simple answer like "Fine."

Mr. Martel went on to describe a mass (lump) on her neck that they noticed in Quebec. They took her to their vet there, who just looked at it and promptly told them it was nothing to worry about. Mr. Martel then went on to tell me that Solie used to get hamburgers from the drive-through, but now she can't tolerate them anymore. Just then Mrs. Martel lifted her head up and interrupted him.

160

"Yeah, she had a nasty bout of vomiting in Quebec this summer. *Our* vet gave us some pills and sent us home. He told us no more hamburgers and we figured we might as well just feed her dog food. He does things a little different than you do down here. He seems more practical. I don't think he's ever had to do any tests on her to figure anything out. He just knows," she said referring to the time I once hospitalized Solie on IV fluids for pancreatitis. That time it had also been due to the drive-through.

I had given up trying to talk to them about the lump and the table food years ago. The mass they had 'just noticed,' had been there for over three years. I had actually biopsied and diagnosed it as a benign fatty tumor known as Lipoma. My medical advice years ago had been to remove it. As with the advice about the table food, they ignored it and then forgot all about it.

Melissa tried to unhook Solie from the leash that Mr. Martel had tied to the bench. He had tied a knot that even the most avid sailor couldn't unravel. When she bent down, Solie went to the end of the leash and hid under the bench.

"Now, honey, you've got to go slow with Solie. She isn't partial to all this…this vet business!" Mr. Martel instructed her, as he pushed her arm out of the way. He unhooked the leash himself and handed Solie to Melissa.

During the exam, Solie constantly squirmed in an attempt to free herself from Melissa. She was frantically running in place, thinking if she ran hard enough she'd be free. In addition, during my exam, she would cry out every time I physically touched her. Mrs. Martel, in turn, would audibly gasp, as she rocked back and forth on the bench. The entire time, Mr. Martel sat staring at me while he rubbed Mrs. Martel's back.

Thankfully, she was only due her rabies vaccination. When I arrived at that final portion of the program, I asked Mrs. Martel if she wanted us to take Solie back to the treatment area. I was referencing the last time when Solie had got a vaccine and screeched out in response. Mrs.

Martel had subsequently screamed out, "Dear Lord, how rough are you?!" and then immediately started crying. She had got so upset that it had taken all of Jen's skills to comfort her. When Jen had offered her a few tissues, she wound up taking the actual box of tissues home with her.

"No, Doctor, you can do it here. I can handle it. I promise. Just let me know when you give the vaccine so I don't have to look," Mrs. Martel meekly responded.

It's not uncommon for people to have a needle phobia or have an aversion to seeing their pet get an injection. I empathize with them, and we have a large demographic of clients who I'll notify in advance. But Mrs. Martel takes it to a whole new level, and I knew already she'd break her promise.

For the most part, the majority of pets don't actually notice or respond when getting an injection. However, some do notice. There is no pattern on which pet will react or how they will react. I have seen little chihuahuas seem to be unaffected, and likewise, large stereotypically 'tougher' breeds cry out in response. I already knew what Solie was going to do.

"OK, Mrs. Martel, it will only be a few seconds. One-two-three, all done—"

Solie let out a loud crying bark that sounded more like a screech. Afterward, she continued with multiple high-pitch barks. She went on long after I had finished with the actual injection.

"It's OK, Solie. It's all over. You'll be OK. It wasn't *that* bad," Melissa said, trying her best to help the situation. With any other client that would be a solid response but with the Martels, apparently, that was exactly the wrong response.

"You didn't get the vaccine! How do you know? Do you like getting a needle jabbed in ya?! Come here, Solie," Mr. Martel barked, as he took her from Melissa's arms. Mrs. Martel was doubled over sitting on the bench with her head between her legs and audibly sobbing.

Mrs. Martel chimed in with her response muffled. "Oh, my! She is never that way with Dr. Leclerc. Never!"

"It will be OK, Solie. I was studying to be a nurse actually, and in people, it goes in the muscle, that one is just under the skin—" Melissa stated, directing her response at Solie, who was cradled in Mr. Martel's arms.

"Well, obviously it hurt her! You ever seen a person scream and cry like that after getting a shot? I haven't! Let's go, honey!" Mr. Martel said helping Mrs. Martel up with his free hand. As they walked out of the exam room, Mrs. Martel was rifling through her purse for tissues. Mr. Martel looked at me one last time as I handed him the entire box of tissues. He grabbed the box and then shook his head as he went through the door.

"A rough day huh, Solie? That mean doctor give you a nasty vaccine? It's all over and you can go home and relax now," I could hear Liz say, as they made their way up front. It was her classic line that she'd jokingly used a thousand times. With the Martels, however, they most likely perceived it as true, and it only further added insult to my injury.

Melissa stood motionless with a blank expression on her face. She was waiting for my reaction as if she had made a mistake and was waiting for the impending reprimand. I waved her off, shook my head in response, and gave her a smirk. I then rolled my eyes and smiled. I was trying to put her at ease. I was reluctant to actually say anything, knowing the Martels could hear us with the open exam-room door.

I grabbed the chart and headed into the treatment area, anxious to discuss what had happened. Before I could say anything, Jen stopped me. She was holding my next appointment's record in her hand.

"That wasn't so bad, was it? See, I knew Melissa could handle it. You think you need me for everything. You need to get used to it. One day I'll be retired, and these girls are going to have to step their game up… Come on, Dr. Miller, this one is a walk-in emergency. I'll go in with you this time. Happy now?"

Without stopping and explaining the appointment, Jen walked into the next exam room. She then motioned me to follow behind her. As soon I went through the door she handed me the chart. When I saw Tony Ryan's muzzle, I immediately knew what was wrong with him.

His owner, Lisa Ryan, was leaning against the wall and looking down at her phone. Her black hair stopped at her shoulders. She was wearing a long, plain white T-shirt, black jeans, and white converse all-stars. She had on a pair of thick, black-rimmed glasses, and tunnel earrings that stretched a hole in her earlobes. Aside from her freckles, she was almost unrecognizable from the girl who barely reached the exam table years ago. No matter how many times I see her, my mind has difficulty coming to terms with the current older version. To accept it, I would have to admit that I was actually aging as well.

"Hey, Dr. Miller, how are you doing?" she greeted me as she placed her phone into her purse.

"Good. How's your mom doing?" I asked, knowing that they had lost Mr. Ryan to a stroke months earlier. He had been another one of our favorite clients. He'd had a great sense of humor and excelled at talking trash to the entire staff. He'd been originally from Boston and would take pride in giving me a hard time about anything to do with New York City, especially when it came to sports. It seemed that every time he'd had an appointment, another one of my teams had taken a hit in some way or another. I will always remember him asking, "How 'bout them Yankees, baby!?" in his thick Boston accent.

"She's fine. Doing really well actually. But we all still miss Dad. He was one of a kind that's for sure," she replied.

"We all miss him. Mr. Ryan was a trip. He was one of my favorite clients, and I don't like anyone," Jen added without missing a beat.

Lisa laughingly responded, "That sounds like something my dad would say. He was always such a wise ass."

"I know, that's why we all loved him here. He fit right in," Jen said kneeling down next to Tony.

Tony was a three-year-old black, flat-coated retriever. When I looked down at him, he resembled more of a chow. His muzzle, eyelids, and head were completely swollen. His body was covered in small hives, and even his front paws appeared swollen. Despite looking miserable, he was still friendly and engaging. He enthusiastically wagged his tail the entire time, and if you mistakenly got close enough, he would spring toward you and try to lick you.

"When did you first notice all this?" I said, bending down as I started my exam.

"He was out running in the yard this morning like always, and then when he came back in, his face looked slightly swollen. It wasn't obvious but within, like, a couple of hours he looked like that. That's when I called and Liz told me to bring him right over. What do you think did that?"

"I know he's having an allergic reaction. But we usually never figure out exactly what causes it. Aside from his swelling, everything is normal," I said, finishing his exam.

"Weird. You think he could have been bitten by a snake? I've seen snakes out in the yard before. I know I saw one last night."

"Did you see what color it was?" I asked, kneeling back down to double check my exam. Jen, who had already stood up, flashed me her classic look of disapproval for having to carry out yet another exam.

"I don't really remember what it looked like exactly. It was kind of …black. Maybe two feet…"

"I don't see any puncture wounds, he doesn't seem painful anywhere... Did you notice any puncture wounds? He wasn't limping... was he?" I asked, as I carefully finished going through his thick hair coat looking for any puncture wounds.

I stood back up, reached in my pocket, and pulled out my phone. I figured I'd let technology be my friend and see if I could get a positive ID on the snake. One of the more common snakes we come across is the southern black racer, and it's non-venomous. I stood next to her showing her the screen as I typed. I was preoccupied with talking with her about the snake, and apparently typing too fast.

Instead of typing '*black* racer' in the image search bar, I typed '*back* racer.' I then inadvertently hit the auto-suggestion for what must have been 'racerback bra.' Instantly, my screen was plastered with all sorts of images of women modeling bras. Making matters worse, one specific image in the center had a model wearing a bra along with matching panties.

Embarrassed, I quickly tried to close the screen but instead clicked on one of the images, enlarging it instead. Fumbling around, I finally managed to close the screen. I felt my face flush. After an awkwardly long pause, I tried to recover and joked, "Let's try that one again..."

Now shaken, I struggled to type as I desperately tried to avoid any mistakes on the second go around. My mind was already trying to determine if she had watched the screen as I had typed the first time. I was starting to think that she hadn't specifically witnessed it for herself. This would leave her to wonder, what exactly her beloved family vet was getting into on his phone during his free time.

Finally, my phone's screen was now covered in images of the beloved southern black racer.

"Yeah. I guess that kind of looks like it. It was dark. I don't always pay attention that closely. I hate snakes. You think this is a snake bite?"

"I don't think it is. Usually, those will have a localized painful swelling with a puncture wound in the middle. If that is the type of snake you usually see, then they are harmless."

"What did all this then?" she asked.

"I think it's an allergic reaction. What actually caused it, I won't be able to tell you. It could be anything. Dogs more commonly get anaphylactoid reactions. These are usually mild reactions like what I think Tony has. Anaphylactic reactions, on the other hand, are the more serious life-threatening ones. A lot of the time they'll vomit first. Their cardiovascular and respiratory systems go into shock. If they aren't treated immediately, those reactions can be fatal. They don't usually get hives and swelling. If they do, it progresses over minutes, not hours like Tony. I am going to go ahead and draw up a couple of injections to treat Tony. Then I will probably keep him here to keep an eye on him." The entire time, all I could think about were the embarrassing images on my phone.

Jen exited the room to get up a consent form as soon as I mentioned he was staying. I answered a couple more questions and went over his treatment plan. When I left to draw up his injections, Jen traded places with me and made her way back into the exam room. I didn't have a chance to ask my burning question but Jen answered it for me as she went into the exam room. Turning to me as she passed, she whispered, "Nice phone!"

Moments later, she returned with Tony and the signed form. I gave him two injections in the muscles along his back; an antihistamine and a steroid. He was a perfect patient for both and, unlike Solie, acted like nothing had happened. As Jen was giving him a treat, I asked, "How did you actually see my phone? That's what I want to know."

"I see everything, Dr. Miller. How long have we been working together? And you don't know that by now. I want to know how a black racer snake search brings up women in lingerie. Explain what you typed for that. Or was that some previous search on your phone?" she asked or started what felt like an interrogation.

"Come on, man, I was searching for pictures of the snake. You didn't watch me type that in?" I responded trying to sound confident and hoping to blow her off.

"How am I going to read text from far away like that? But I could see all those pictures though. Show me how that even comes up," she challenged back.

Frantically, I tried over and over to replicate the search on my phone. Each time images of the black racer snake appeared. I even tried a different search engine and a couple of misspellings without any luck. I knew I would have to remain on Jen's good side for the entire rest of the day.

It would allow me to cut through her gruff facade and make my appeal to the virtuous and kind nature that lived deep below the surface. Only then would I be able to maintain my innocence and get her honest opinion on any lasting effects on Lisa Ryan. For now, I'd have to ride it out.

"Hey, Dr. Miller, quit playing with your phone! Isn't that what got you into trouble in the first place? Your next one is here. And don't worry…Melissa can handle Mr. Taylor," Jen said as she gave Melissa a subtle wink.

9:45 am

Sean Taylor was standing in the exam room when I walked in. He was wearing a blue dress shirt, with the sleeves rolled up to his forearms, and dark-blue dress pants. His black hair was slicked back and parted to one side. His beard showed about a day of growth. With his black hair, blue eyes, and all-American jawline, I always joked to the staff that he looked like Clark Kent. Jen would be quick to add in and correct me, "Yeah, maybe if Clark Kent was a model for Abercrombie and Fitch!"

He was yet another client whose appearance highlighted my short stature as well as my age. He was a physician's assistant at a nearby

168

hospital. He was always friendly, laid back, and extremely easy to deal with. Unlike some medical professionals we get, Mr. Taylor didn't give us the third degree over every diagnosis and treatment. He took the other approach and went along with what we told him, only asking a few well-thought-out and reasonable questions.

Diane Taylor was lying on her chest with her head between her front legs. She looked like a motionless pile of red hair laid out on the floor. She resembled a skinny golden retriever, with curly poodle hair and a muzzle that resembled a standard poodle. Even after I'd come into the exam room and started talking, she'd remained perfectly still. I could already tell she was ill. She was a far cry from the extremely boisterous and outgoing four-year-old Labradoodle we were used to seeing.

The Labradoodle is the OG (original gangster) 'designer' dog. It was bred in an attempt to create a hypoallergenic dog for people, by mating a Labrador retriever with a poodle. Unfortunately, there is no such thing as a hypoallergenic dog. Most Labradoodles have some common traits but their appearance and behavioral characteristics are all different. Nonetheless, they remain popular and are still unrecognized by the AKC; if you're keeping purebred score.

"Hey, Dr. Miller, how are you doing?" Mr. Taylor asked as he extended his hand.

"Hanging in there, man. Good to see you," I said shaking his hand. "I can already see Diane is not herself today."

"I know. She's been like that all weekend. No other symptoms, just really lethargic and not really interested in eating," he answered in a soft-spoken tone that lacked any geographical clues as to where he was originally from.

My exam was as unrewarding as the medical history. Despite her obviously being depressed, her only other abnormality was that her abdomen felt tense. Even though Diane didn't have the classic signs of pancreatitis like vomiting and diarrhea, it could still fit with the lethargy and possible mild abdominal pain.

"You sure she couldn't have eaten anything… out of her normal diet? Anything she might have got by accident?" I had already asked about table food but I was giving him another out to come clean. Pancreatitis isn't always caused by table food but in our practice, it's a common culprit.

"No, not that I can think of. My little nephew was over on Saturday and he might have slipped her something…but I don't think he did. She was already starting to act lethargic then. Usually, she is all excited when he comes over. She was kind of laid back on Saturday."

I was holding out hope that this case was going to be business as usual and it was pancreatitis. Except, this time, I wasn't convinced and the lab work was going to be my backup plan to get some more clues. I decided to send Diane's blood work, a pancreas test, and urinalysis to the lab. I also decided to send Diane home with a prescription GI (gastrointestinal) diet, just in case.

I had Melissa bring in a sample of the diet on a paper plate. I wanted to see if I could entice Diane with canned food and check her appetite. She inhaled it. After she licked the plate clean she looked up to Mr. Taylor as if he'd be the one to give her some more.

"Typical. She doesn't eat this morning and then acts like she's starving here. She's trying to make me look like a hypochondriac," Mr. Taylor commented in response.

"You're no hypochondriac, trust me. I'm not surprised she ate the canned food, especially since she's normally on dry food. It's obvious she's not her normal self. I'm glad we're checking her lab work," I replied.

"She probably got into something. It wouldn't surprise me. It makes sense with the abdominal pain. I can't possibly see what else it could be," Mr. Taylor replied, agreeing where many clients would probably start to argue.

After he left with Diane, I already had a feeling it was going to be a difficult case. In hindsight, however, I really had no clue how much of challenge getting a diagnosis was actually going to be. I wouldn't have to wait long on the lab work. I'd get that answer early. It returned after I finished discharging Tony Ryan.

4:50 pm

Tony did well. His swelling responded dramatically to medication. Except for the left side of his muzzle having some residual swelling, he was completely back to normal. When I went over his oral medications (antihistamines and steroids) with Lisa Ryan I had difficulty concentrating. All I could think about was trying to read her reaction. I was determined to find out if I now had a fractured client relationship on my hands. Making matters worse, I've never been comfortable still calling her Lisa.

I always try to keep up professional appearances. At least with the outside world of clients and specialists. As far as my staff are concerned, that's a different story. I don't advocate having an entire staff who are unconventional, independent, and borderline dysfunctional but it's always worked out well for me.

I had been seeing Lisa Ryan since she was a child, and with that, along with the age difference, I wasn't able to bring myself to address her as Mrs. Ryan. She'd always be Lisa. She was one of the few clients I called by their first name. To me, she represented a preview of when I'd be older, and there would be many more first names.

"Lisa, it could have been anything. Something he ate that he wasn't supposed to, an insect bite, anything. It's just like we discussed this morning. I know it's an allergic reaction but what exactly he was exposed to that caused it, I won't be able to tell you. I can tell you that it's not a snake bite," I said, answering her question and desperately still trying to read the situation.

"Thank God for that. It was pretty scary. I really appreciate it, thank—"

As per usual and as if on cue, Melissa came in with Tony pulling on the leash. His front legs were beating against the floor but he was making little progress at the end of his leash. When he finally got close to her, he leaped up on Lisa, and almost knocked her down.

Lisa then became focused on Tony. "Did you miss me, baby?"

Melissa took the bottles of medication from the exam table and handed them to her along with Tony's leash. Lisa thanked me again and left. I still hadn't been able to figure out her take of the 'back racer bra' search on my phone.

When I left the exam room, Jen was already in exit mode. She had her handbag over her shoulder and her sunglasses resting on her head. It was one of those Mondays when Jen knew she could make a timely exit, and she was determined to be the first one to leave.

"See you all tomorrow. Diane's blood work is back and it's not pancreatitis. Goodnight, sir!"

I looked over the lab work, and as Jen had already clued me in on, it was completely normal. I called Mr. Taylor but I got his voicemail.

"It's Dr. Miller. We got back Diane's lab work, and it's all completely normal. I'll give you a call in the morning and touch base with you then. Have a good evening."

Tuesday 8:25 am

I arrived early on Tuesday morning. I was anxious to show Jen that I had finally cracked the code. I pulled my phone out and showed her the exact missteps that landed me on a screen filled with women in lingerie. I was proud of my accomplishment and it made the lengthy explanation to my wife the night before totally worth it. Jen wasn't at all impressed.

"Dr. Miller, first of all, Uh, *good morning* by the way. I can't believe you are still on that. Really? Are you serious? You were worried about that? Come on, Dr. Miller, we were messing with you. You really thought that we all think you've got some kind of freaky stuff on your phone? That's a good one. Let's just say you had that sort of thing on your phone, I'm not a guy, but I'd think the woman would be like…like completely naked. I mean if you were looking at that, would you really be looking at women in their underwear? Really, Dr. Miller. Please, don't start. I don't need to be tortured all day with what little Lisa may, or may not, be thinking about."

"You don't think that might be important? Well, what *do* you think?" I was finally off the hook with the staff but I was still clueless on Lisa Ryan.

Jen took a long pause before she answered. She ignored me at first and remained focused on a breakfast sandwich that she thought was more deserving of her attention. It was obvious she was trying to convey that I had disturbed her precious few minutes of personal time before appointments started.

"Dr. Miller, I don't know what answer you're looking for. I can't read people's minds, and that applies to women as well. But—"

The treatment area phone made a loud beep interrupting Jen. It was Liz on the speaker. "Dr. Miller, it's Mr. Taylor on line two."

I picked up the phone.

"Hey, Dr. Miller, good morning. Any news on the blood work?" Mr. Taylor was off to an early start calling me first, and that made me worry that Diane had got worse.

"No news, or no bad news anyway. The lab work and pancreas test are all normal. The urine is on the dilute side of normal but other than that it's all normal. How did Diane do overnight?"

"She likes that canned food. Her appetite is OK. I'd say she's improved slightly… but she is still pretty depressed. She is nowhere

173

near her old self. I just can't put my finger on it. What do you think is wrong with her?" he asked in his usual soft-spoken tone but I could tell he was worried. He was looking for a definitive answer and I didn't have it.

"I think the lab work rules out quite a bit but there are still other things that could be going on that wouldn't show up on lab work." I went on to discuss a laundry list of differential diagnoses. All were possible but none were definitive. My top two were an occult UTI and tick-borne disease (like Lyme disease). Despite the fact that tick-borne diseases are supposed to be on the rise in Florida, they still aren't as common as in other regions of the country. Furthermore, I have definitively diagnosed only three cases in my practice.

"What's the next step?" he asked, putting an end to my waffling.

"Good question…" I inadvertently blurted out loud. I quickly restarted, as if to try cover for what I'd said. "If she is still lethargic tomorrow, I'd like to see her back and take X-rays. If those are normal, then I'd recommend a urine culture, and maybe a blood test to screen for tick-borne diseases."

"X-rays? What are you looking for?"

As a physician's assistant, he had been following along closely and knew that the test would be looking for something I hadn't yet mentioned.

"Even though she is young and juvenile, and cancer is relatively rare in veterinary medicine, I want to have a look and rule out that there isn't a mass or tumor." Cancer was low on my list, but it needed to be ruled out. The other two tests would take days to return, and X-rays would immediately give us results. It would give me a basic look inside her chest and abdomen. So, I prioritized the X-rays, even though I was starting to doubt they'd reveal what was wrong with Diane.

When I got off the phone with Mr. Taylor, I was hoping that Diane would turn around overnight. It would put an end to the diagnostic nightmare I already knew would be waiting for me. He called back Wednesday afternoon and told Liz that Diane had stopped eating even the canned food. He decided to drop Diane off on Thursday morning. I already knew things were about to get complicated.

Thursday 9:00 am

"Let me know if those are OK?" Jen asked me as I looked over Diane's radiographs. They represented Melissa's second attempt at taking Diane's X-rays.

"The abdomen is good but the chest is still a little too light. They'll need to redo those again," I replied as I started to look over the X-rays of her abdomen.

"See, sir, this is what happens without me. It's like I have to do everything around here. When I retire you are going to be in real trouble, trust me," Jen said as she walked toward radiology to offer her encouraging words of wisdom to Cassey and Melissa.

As I continued to look at the films, I could hear tidbits from Jen in radiology.

"Those settings are off. No wonder they are still too light. Melissa, I'm going to show you one more time where to measure the chest. You should know all this by now. It hasn't changed since the last time you worked here, or the last time we took films together."

It was obvious that the honeymoon period with Melissa was over. Jen had come to grips with the fact, just like last time, that Melissa would perpetually be 'in training.' Rather than alleviating Jen's workload, like Jen had initially fantasized, she was adding to it.

Diane's X-rays were completed, with Jen's input, and they were normal. Since she had been dropped off while I had been in my first appointment, I hadn't had a chance to re-examine her. When Melissa brought her over to me, I looked over her record, and she had lost four pounds since her last visit. She shuffled along and looked even more depressed than on Monday. Her abdomen was still tense, and now she had a fever. Her temperature was 105.9 (normal is 101.5).

With no diagnosis and the weekend fast approaching, I knew what decision I had to make. But first I had to talk to Mr. Taylor. I called his cell, and he answered on the first ring.

"It's Dr. Miller. I had a look at Diane's films, and they're all normal. I just finished examining her, and I'm concerned because she's lost four pounds since Monday, and now she has a fever of 105.9. I don't want her to go through the weekend like this, and I think our next move is to refer her to the specialist."

"Wow, 105? That's crazy. Man...I absolutely agree, we need an answer. I'm at work but, if I need to boot out of here early, I can. Any idea what could be going on with her? This whole thing is really bizarre."

"I actually don't have any new ideas, other than what we discussed. It could still be a tick-borne disease, or an infection somewhere, like her abdomen. Her abdomen still appears pretty painful. But it's a hard case to piece together. I'm at the end of the diagnostic tests that we can do here and get an immediate answer. That's why I want her to go to the specialist. I'm going to try and see if they can get her in this afternoon."

"Cool. Thanks, Dr. Miller. I really appreciate it. Let me know as soon as you find out when I need to be there."

Mr. Taylor was one of those medical professionals who made my life easier. With his underlying medical knowledge, he understood the need for specialist intervention. He also emphatically trusted what I recommended without question. Ironically, the need for a specialist, in this case, is something that I myself would later question.

When I called the specialists, I was transferred to Kristen Nichols. She was an internal-medicine specialist but had only been in private practice for a few years. I remember going to one of her lectures at a conference several years ago when she had just finished her residency. Back then, she had been petite and had long blonde hair. She'd looked like she was barely in college never mind being a specialist. She's done a great job on all the cases I've ever referred to her. My clients always rave about her. Their compliments never surprise me because she is always gracious and friendly. And, by the way, extremely energetic.

"Hey, Dr. Miller, whatcha got going on for me?!"

"Hey, Dr. Nichols, I got a classic ADR. It's a four-year-old spayed Labradoodle not eating. Blood work and X-rays all normal, today her temp was a hundred and five..." ADR (ain't doing right) is a classic veterinary term. It refers to a case where the patient is lethargic but showing no other obvious signs or symptoms. Thus, prompting the owner, back in the day, to tell their old country vet, "Doc, it just ain't doing right." That response caught on, and now it's a legit medical vet term.

I went on to regurgitate Diane's history of the last few days, and as always, I felt like I was droning on too long and giving too much information. Just as I was about to finish, she cut me off confirming my suspicion.

"Sounds like we need to see her. That's a tough one. No problem, Dr. Miller. We have a slot at three-thirty. Think you could have her here by then?" she replied on what sounded like the same breath. Before I could ask what she thought was wrong with Diane, she was gone. It wasn't until the next day that I got her answer. And as with most referrals, the information came in the form of a faxed letter.

Friday 8:32 am

When I walked into the treatment area, I was greeted by Jen holding three pieces of paper stapled together.

"I know what you're gonna say, 'I could've done that, and we should have done that here.' I don't want to hear it today. So, don't

177

start. I'm going to give you a compliment. I don't say this often and don't make me take it back. You're a good vet, and you made the right call. OK. Happy? Now, I don't want to hear any crap about this case all day and ruin my Friday. Don't make me take back my compliment. So, before I hand you this, promise me! Promise?"

I promised.

OWNER: Sean Taylor

PATIENT: Diane

Dear Dr. Miller,

Diane presented for continued evaluation of decreased appetite and lethargy. Her physical examination revealed an elevated temperature (105.9F) and an intermittently tense abdomen. An abdominal ultrasound was unremarkable. We have submitted a tick panel (pending) and have started Doxycycline.

Thank you for your confidence in this referral. If we can provide any further information regarding this case, please do not hesitate to contact us.

Kind Regards,

K. Nichols

Kristen Nichols, DVM, DACVIM

I didn't bother reading the detailed play by play and case notes on the next two pages. As soon I made it to the end of the letter, I was immediately taken back to my final year in vet school in Edinburgh.

After diagnosing what appeared to be a challenging case, the clinician on our rotation would inevitably say, "See, this case *seemed* complicated but had the referring vet taken the time and stuck to basic principles, they could have done all this themselves. This case really didn't need to be referred, did it? You could all have done this yourselves. And in practice, you will do these yourselves. My days here won't be as busy once you lot graduate."

Still, I kept my promise to Jen. It was one of those rare days that Jen flipped her script. She went out of her way to remain upbeat. Instead of using her witty sense of humor for her typical comebacks, she employed it to crack jokes in an effort to cheer me up.

Liz called Mr. Taylor that afternoon for an update, and he said Diane was already starting to improve. By the time the end of the day rolled around, I was glad the day, week, and that case were finally over. Of course, that case wasn't really over.

Diane's Definitive Diagnosis

Monday Afternoon

I had finished my morning appointments and was about to head out for lunch when <Beep!> Liz came over the speakerphone. "Dr. Miller, it's Dr. Nichols on line one, about Diane…"

I picked up the phone.

"Hey, Dr. Miller. I just got off the phone with Mr. Taylor. We got back Diane's tick panel and it was negative. He said she had improved initially but since Sunday she's still kind of ADR and her appetite is still off. Even though the tick panel was negative, I'd like to continue the Doxycycline. We were going to have Mr. Taylor come back and see us but, because of his schedule, he can't get in till Thursday. I was wondering if you'd be able to see her and grab us a urine culture. To kind of speed things up." She still sounded upbeat and confident, despite the fact that this case had now become even more complicated.

"Yeah, we can get him tomorrow. I'm surprised. I was convinced it would be positive. Even so, I figured whatever infection she had was responding to the doxy—"

She cut me off before I finished.

"Oh, one last thing, I almost forgot. If you could *please* grab some films of her back that would be a huge help. I want to check for disko. It was another thing I thought of that would fit. This way I can have the radiologist check them out before Thursday."

Diskospondylitis is an infection in the disk space between the vertebrae.

"Yeah, that'd be OK. Normally she'd be hyper and we'd have to sedate her for all this. But as lethargic as she's been, we should be able to grab all that pretty easily. No problem. I'll email the films."

"Hey, you guys are awesome. I really appreciate it! I'll keep you posted. I bet you're glad you referred this one now. Take care and thanks!" It was as if she'd read my mind, and before I could answer she was gone.

"Well, well, well, Dr. Miller. Looks like I was right again about that referral. Not so simple is it? I'm glad we have to do all the legwork. How come the specialists can't do their own tests?" As usual, Jen had been listening closely to my phone call.

"Come on, man, veterinarian medicine is a team sport. Haven't you heard there is no 'I' in team," I fired back.

"Hahaha, that's a good one, Dr. Miller. There is an 'I' in intern, though, and that's what we're like, the specialists' interns. As far as the team is concerned, we know *you* won't be taking any X-rays. But, don't worry, we'll get it all done tomorrow. Go enjoy your lunch, sir," she said quickly, trying to finish before I walked out.

Tuesday

Because of a schedule change at his hospital, Mr. Taylor had to move his appointment with Dr. Nichols to Friday. When we saw Diane on Tuesday, her weight was up a pound, but she was visibly depressed, and looking pretty miserable. She was far removed from her normal happy, hyper self. She also still had a fever of 104.9. At that point, I was starting to worry that whatever was going on was getting worse. I was starting to feel anxious, especially since their appointment now wasn't until Friday.

'I' was in the team on that particular Tuesday, because Melissa had called in sick and Cassey was on vacation. That left me to assist Jen with getting samples and performing tests on all the patients that day. I had to fill in the part of technician and, as always, thankfully I make a better veterinarian than I do a tech. This role reversal isn't lost on Jen, and she takes pleasure in reminding me how little I know about their job. Especially when it came to taking Diane's X-rays.

"That's not straight, Dr. Miller. More to the left. My left! These films are going to the specialist. You don't want us to look like a derelict practice, do you? I'd like to see you do this with Melissa. I'd pay to see that. Imagine if *I* called in sick? You would have to reschedule this or tell the specialist to do— You have to push the peddle all the way down, hard!" There was a beep from the X-ray machine. "Finally! Let's see how that one comes out…"

Under Jen's direction, the films came out perfect. I glanced at them and couldn't see any obvious abnormalities. I knew, however, that specific diagnosis would take the trained eye of a specialist. Of course, so did Jen. "Dr. Miller, the next appointment is here and I need your help. Stop trying to waste time looking at those X-rays. You have no idea what you're looking at anyway. You can't stall and wait for someone else to become available to help today 'cause today that someone is you!" she said, laughing at her own joke.

I already appreciate my staff but, on that day, if Jen was looking to put me in the technician trenches, she got her wish. I was reminded firsthand what it's like getting scratched up and having pets scream in your ear just because they want no part of something simple, like just being held. For good measure, I had a cute little nervous Schnauzer named Lacey, completely express her anal glands on me when I took her temperature. As always, that backup scrub top I keep meaning to bring in was still at home.

For the last appointment, I had to wear an old maroon scrub top that we had lying around. And it didn't exactly match the faded blue pants I was wearing. That wasn't the real problem, however, as this particular scrub top was as far from being gender neutral as you could get. To say it was a more feminine version would be an understatement. The pink trim on the collar and the tight fit weren't helping matters much either.

When I complained to Jen, she had no sympathy.

"Maybe now you'll bring in a scrub for yourself. How about you at least let me order you one? But we both know none of that's going to happen, don't we? You have one last appointment, what are you worried about? That, what, one person is going to notice poor Dr. Miller in his little cute top?"

That appointment wasn't just one person, like Jen predicted, it was actually two. Connor and Megan Johnson were both in their early twenties. They were also new clients. That was their first appointment with their new Great Dane puppy, Gemma. After I awkwardly introduced myself, I was looking for an opening through the entire appointment, to explain the scrub top, but it never came.

Any hope for a quick exit was also squashed after a constant barrage of new-puppy questions came my way. Toward the end, I found it difficult to concentrate, as they both had smiles planted on their faces, which was in no doubt from that scrub top.

After it was all finally over, I was so pissed off at the scrub top I took it off and slammed it in the laundry bin, leaving me to finish writing the record up in my white T-shirt. I was getting ready to leave when Liz came back with a record and put it in the holder on the exam-room door.

Jen looked over at me and teased, "Not so fast. You are going to have to put that cute little top on one last time. You have to discharge Mr. Taylor. You may not have any results but he's got some questions. You can also let him know that we offered Diane the canned venison food, and she ate it all up today. He may want to take some home."

I grabbed the scrub top out of the laundry bin and struggled to put it back on. In my new-found hate for this particular scrub top, I tore the seam under the left armpit, exposing my white T-shirt. Before I could even ask, Jen, noticing my plight, responded, "Nice! That was the last one for you. The other ones we got are all pink and purple, and definitely won't fit."

"I'd keep that left arm down," she added, as I grabbed the chart and went into the room.

Looking at Mr. Taylor, I was implicitly reminded of my situation. He was dressed in gray dress pants, a light blue dress shirt, and a red tie. His black hair was parted to the side, without a strand out of place. Perfectly resembling both a fashion model and a dead ringer for Clark Kent.

"How's it going?" he asked.

"Rough day today. I lost my scrub top to a medically related incident. And now I gotta wear this one," I replied holding up the pink trim for added effect. This time, I wasn't going to wait to clarify my new dress code.

"Yeah, that sucks. I can relate to that. I can always grab a spare scrub top at the hospital, though. You should keep a few here." He paused as if waiting for an excuse as to why I didn't have one before continuing, "Could you see anything on the films?"

"I couldn't see anything, no. But I'd like to hear what the specialists say once they get a chance to read them."

"I'm going to try and get off work to see Dr. Nichols before Friday but any new ideas? I'm starting to get a little worried here about her," he asked, the level of concern in his voice was apparent.

"I can tell you she still has a fever, and it's obvious she's still pretty depressed. I have no new ideas as to what's causing all this, and I'm at loss for a diagnosis at this point. I'm glad that you took her to the specialist, and hopefully, you can get there before Friday—"

"Here's your daddy!" Jen exclaimed, leading Diane into the room. Diane perked up slightly. But it appeared as if she was in slow motion, as she wagged her tail and tried to close the distance between the doorway and Mr. Taylor. Mr. Taylor took the leash from Jen, thanked me, and left.

I took the scrub top off and this time I pitched it straight in the garbage. I didn't know if it could be repaired and I didn't care. I left that evening feeling that I had let Mr. Taylor down. I was worried that something drastic would happen with Diane before he was able to go back for his next appointment.

That Next Appointment

Mr. Taylor was unable to get off earlier and didn't see Dr. Nichols until Friday. It was a long three days, and I called him on both Wednesday and Thursday morning. Both times, I had a nervous apprehension that Mr. Taylor would tell me something I didn't want to hear about Diane. However, both times he told me she was about the same and still continuing to eat the venison.

I didn't call him on Friday morning and was anxiously awaiting Dr. Nichols' call. It finally arrived.

Friday 2:05 pm

<Beep!>

"Dr. Miller, it's Dr. Nichols on line two for—" Liz exclaimed. I grabbed the phone before she could finish.

"Hey, Dr. Miller. Thank you so much for getting those tests done. They were a huge help. Nothing really to see on the films. Diane came back to see us today and it's now pretty clear. Well, I think so anyway. I guess we'll have to see if I'm right. She still has the fever, 104.7 today but she developed new signs. Mr. Taylor said she started limping last night and she was visibly limping on her right forelimb here this morning. Both her elbow joints are swollen and painful. We tapped them and I'm sending the fluid in for a culture and analysis. I'm fairly confident she's got immune-mediated polyarthritis. So, if the culture is negative, I'll probably be starting her on steroids on Monday. Then I'm going to have him recheck with you guys in two weeks. If she is doing well, we can talk about lowering her dose. I'm finishing up the formal report now with all the details and you should have it by tonight. I'll call you when the culture comes back. Thanks."

As soon as I thanked her, she was gone.

Dr. Nichols was right. Diane's joint-fluid analysis came back suggestive of immune-mediated polyarthritis, and the culture was negative. On Monday afternoon, she was started on steroids. The following Wednesday, Mr. Taylor called Liz to get more venison and told her Diane had already started to improve and was like a new dog.

When I saw her back two weeks later she was back to her old self. She was so hyper that it took three people to recheck her blood work. Unfortunately, I couldn't help out on that one. I was, of course, too busy. I had to call Dr. Nichols. I left Jen to get Melissa to help her and Cassey. I still haven't brought in that backup scrub top.

The Exodus of Esposito

I told you it was only a matter of time. Of course, you thought we made it this far and that maybe she'd slipped through the cracks. Perhaps we had a change of heart, once we took a pause and viewed things a bit more clearly. She did give us that delicious cake. She even told Liz she made it herself, and that you could taste the love in every bite. I will admit, all of the slices I ate (stole from the rest of the staff) represented the best pound cake I've ever eaten.

I'm sorry to have to tell you but she didn't make it in our practice. So, what kind of degenerate vet practice could possibly have an altercation with such a sweet, kind-hearted, and devoted dog owner, you might ask? You're not alone. It's a question most people probably ask after they hear her story. And a lot of people are asking it too. Her story has gained quite of bit of traction. It's been spread around the Jack-A-Poo community and probably even reached New York City. I'm convinced, by now, even a few innocent veterinarians have had to explain to clients they aren't *that* Dr. Miller.

None of them have heard the entire story. They only know what she tells them. She might have a little yellow notepad but she wasn't taking notes on all this. Not to mention that she only writes down what she thinks is important and puts her own spin on things. That alone, was part of the problem. There's more, and don't worry you'll have the complete story behind The Exodus of Ann Marie Esposito. It all started in September. And just like a proper exodus, she left after a plague of sorts that included a hurricane, darkness, and some fleas.

A Hurricane

As far as hurricanes go, the only exposure I had to them growing up was in my grandmother's South Florida condo bathroom. Like most New Yorkers, she migrated there to live out her golden years, and every summer we'd go visit.

Finding myself attending to my business in her bathroom without proper reading material, I'd be forced to read Publix Supermarket's Hurricane Guide. I'm still at loss as to why it was always in the cabinet under the sink, seemingly waiting just for me.

Publix's Hurricane Guide described all the supplies you'd need, and how to stay safe for an actual, real-life hurricane. On the back was a map of South Florida, with a grid imposed on top of it. Before the days of the internet, you could listen to your battery-operated radio (on that supply list) and use the back of this booklet to plot the course of your impending fate.

After I'd flush and return the guide back to its proper resting place, I'd always think, 'I come here every summer and I've never seen any hurricanes. That probably never happens!' That perspective would change years later after Hurricane Andrew devastated South Florida. I gained even more insight when I actually ended up residing in the Sunshine State, and hurricanes actually became a very real threat.

Before Hurricane Irma arrived, our practice had gone through the usual rehearsed phases of preparation. First, there is a risk-assessment phase. In this phase, Jen and I start at least a week before, in order to determine if our practice is in harm's way. Jen not only has a sixth sense for predicting catastrophic events, she also has a hurricane app on her phone, which she swears by. So, when she gave that particular one a 'no damn chance that hits us so, stop asking me!' rating. I felt pretty confident about it.

Despite her more than fifty percent accuracy, which is higher than most meteorologists, she, unfortunately, got that one wrong. By Friday, most all of the predictions had the hurricane headed straight for us and arriving in the wee early hours of Monday morning. This brought us immediately to Phase Two with just three days to go.

Phase Two is a preparation stage, which involves getting things in order for an impending hurricane. When it comes to things like boarding up, there are two types of people in Central Florida: those who do and those who don't. I used to be the former type. I boarded up my home the year we had three hurricanes in a row. I was a worried, new homeowner back then and wanted to do everything by the book. Most of my neighbors, however, did nothing, and all their homes did just fine for all three.

After all that hard work of measuring, cutting, and installing the boards, the wood sat idle in my garage rotting. Five uneventful hurricane seasons later, I finally threw it all out, and proudly joined the non-boarding group. I haven't looked back since. My practice has minimal glass, and for the record, my gamble (laziness) has always paid off there as well.

With the decision not to board pre-determined, the next part of Phase Two is clearing the hospital of any patients. With no power and no guarantee we'd be able to make it in in order to check on them, we clear the practice. The emergency clinic has a large generator and enacts special hours during the hurricane. Any hospitalized patients are transferred. For that particular hurricane, we had no patients.

Next, we started clearing our appointments scheduled for Monday. Generally, that is easy, because most of our clients either suspected the possibility when they made the appointment or were well aware that the storm was coming. Some will actually beat us to it, calling and canceling themselves. However, without fail, there is always one appointment that we can't get hold of, leaving us to wonder if they will actually show up (more on that one later).

Just like with boarding up, when it comes to hurricane preppers in Central Florida, there are two more types of people: those with generators, and those without. I'm in the latter group. As a home, and practice owner, I'm a key decision maker on the budgets for both. My stance has been the same for both, with a solid vote against.

Generators only power a small portion of appliances, they require gasoline to run, and like the boards, usually, sit idle for years. Vital equipment in my practice, like the X-ray machine and the massive air conditioners, can't be powered by a small generator. Getting gas before a hurricane is also a nightmare, and, finally, for most hurricanes, I've got my power back within a couple of days or less. So, again, another hurricane gamble that's paid off.

That brings us to the last and final preparation. With no generator, we have to make provisions for all our perishable drugs, like vaccines, and other drugs that need to be refrigerated. Several hurricanes back, Cassey hooked my practice up. Her father has a generator, and a large fridge in his garage. He agreed to allocate some space for our stuff. It worked out well, at least for us, and I have been taking advantage of that one-sided agreement ever since. For what it's worth, I do see all his pets, and at the employee discount.

He doesn't have space for everything so, we have to pick and choose what to place in his fridge. Balancing between the most expensive and most used, perishable pharmaceuticals, Jen develops a list. And in an effort to double check everything, I always *try* to go over it with her. Her response is always the same.

"Dr. Miller! How many years have I been doing this? Cassey and I will work it out. OK? Just like we do every hurricane. I give her the list of stuff to take. She swings by here before it comes and gets it. The rest she puts in the freezer on ice packs. Maybe if you broke down, and got a generator, we wouldn't have to free-load off her poor dad all the time. But I know, I know your excuse so don't explain it all to me again. Just let me finish making my list. We got this. Trust me. OK?!"

I figured it was pointless to argue with her, and maybe she did have a point about that generator. Besides, up until that hurricane, their record had been perfect. So, I left them to it and went into my two-o'clock appointment with Melissa.

Friday 2:00 pm

Mike and Marshall were sitting next to each other on the exam-room bench when we walked in. Marshall was wearing jeans, a white polo shirt, and brown dress shoes. His hair was parted to the side. Mike is a lawyer and had most likely taken that day off. He was wearing track pants, a T-shirt, and sneakers. He's slightly older than Marshall,

192

roughly in his early fifties. He is also close to a foot shorter than Marshall. After all these years, I still can't get over this difference whenever I see them standing next to one another. Mike's receding black hair is combed straight back. I don't know if it was good genetics or sunbathing but his skin always looks like he just got back from the beach.

As soon as I opened the door, Murray, their English bulldog, ran toward me at full speed. He jumped up on me, and almost knocked me over. By the way, all their pets' names start with an 'M.' It's a tribute to their first names, which they seem to think is pretty cool. I concur.

"Murray! Where are your manners?" Marshall exclaimed. Mike sat looking down at his cell phone and only looked up briefly to shake his head.

Mike Tolbert and Marshall Young are among my favorite clients. They are an institution in our practice. I don't know if they ever officially got married but as far as we are concerned they might as well be. I always try to keep a professional relationship with most of my clients but Mike and Marshall are two that crossed over to the personal side long ago. We see them so frequently, they are two clients who naturally have become like family. Of course, sometimes that can backfire but, that's a story for another (earlier) book.

"Hey, buddy. You miss me? What's going on with Murray?" I asked as I rubbed Murray's head and started to pet him.

"His ears. What else is new? He's been scratching them and shaking his head for the last few days. We wanted to get him in here before the weekend. Oh, for the record, we made this appointment on Monday," Marshall replied, referencing the crowd of people in the waiting area.

Melissa instinctively bent down to hold Murray, while I started his exam.

"Yeah, it's been pretty busy today. You guys ready for this hurricane?" I asked.

"We don't get real hurricanes here. We used to live in Miami and those are real storms. Besides, you know these meteorologists don't know shit!" Marshall replied.

"Language!" Mike interrupted.

Marshall continued, "It's true. Last year they had the storm headed directly for us. Making it all dramatic, like we were all going to die. Then, of course, it turned, and totally missed us. I hate the news! The only prep I'm doing this time is a stiff drink."

As I finished up my exam and stood up, Murray broke free from Melissa. He jumped up and caught me with a nasty, slobbery, bulldog kiss square on my cheek. For good measure, he rubbed his drool on my pant leg. It was as if he was trying to clean himself.

"Aww, so sorry about that, Dr. Miller, but you know Murray loves you," Marshall said, offering a half-hearted apology.

"Yeah, I'm used to that. That's just how Newman used to treat me," I jokingly replied.

"We're… so sorry about Newman. We know you must all still miss him at home. We've been there, that's for sure," Marshall said as I finished making my notes on the record.

"You can borrow Murray if you want. Maybe permanently if he keeps coming in here like this," Mike joked still looking down at his phone.

"Thanks, again. It was good, really good actually. You guys did well with that pick," I replied, referring to a bottle of whiskey they'd dropped off three months back, along with a card, which said, *"Our deepest sympathy. Raise a glass for Newman. We sure will!"*— *Mike and Marshall*

"We knew you'd like it. It's from Scotland. We figure you must know your stuff when it comes to whiskey since you were actually there," Marshall said.

"Yeah, you must have got *some* culture over there and hopefully learned something about real booze," Mike jokingly added.

"Yeah, I did. I learned how to drink it! And there isn't too much left, I can tell you that," I replied getting a good laugh out of both of them.

Murray, it turned out, had a simple ear infection. Pretty routine for all parties involved. So, with the typical 'goody bag' (as Mike calls it) of ear flush and ointment, they were on their way. As usual, after they thanked me, Mike turned to me as he was leaving and joked, "You sure you don't want him?"

4:55 pm (finally)

Whenever a hurricane is coming, many of our clients will panic. They believe that this last day represents their last time to access veterinary care for weeks, if not ever again. This panic opens the floodgates of sick pets, phone calls, and prescription refills. As the day develops, it seems as if these requests grow in frequency and desperation. As fate would have it, the last, and most desperate appointment was Ann Marie Esposito.

"I'm sorry, Dr. Miller. I had no choice. She had to come in now. Wouldn't you rather deal with this now than after the hurricane?" Liz offered, trying to apologize and bargain with me at the same time. She knew I was exhausted and just ready to go home.

When I walked into the exam room, Mrs. Esposito was standing behind the exam table. She was wearing a light blue velour tracksuit and her trademark white golf visor. On the table, she had laid out her little yellow notepad and the top page was filled with notes. JJ was sitting on the floor next to her, patiently waiting at the end of his leash.

"Dr. Millah, thank you so much for getting us in. I'm so worried about JJ, and with the hurricane coming, I thought I wouldn't be able to get in, in time. I didn't want this to get any more advanced."

I glanced down at the record and Liz had simply written "Check skin."

"What's going on with JJ?" I mistakenly asked. Tired from a long day, I was off my game. Rather than asking a specific question, I asked a general one. Way too general, and inadvertently invited her to tell me everything. When she started reading from her pad, I knew I was in trouble.

"I don't even know where to begin. He hasn't been himself all week. He's been taking extra time to finish his food. I think he gets frustrated when he eats because the thing on his hip is bothering him. He's been itching more. He always itches but it seems like now, the thing on his hip is really bothering him. He woke up last night and started to itch and I think it's because the thing on his hip is causing him to be in pain—"

"You say something is on his hip?" I asked, interrupting her, and stepping my game back up.

"Yeah, it's really weird. It came up out of nowhere. Thank goodness the groomer noticed it this morning. His bath was scheduled for next week but I didn't want to take any chances with the hurricane coming."

Melissa, wanting to speed things along, picked up JJ, and placed him on the table. Being the perfect patient he is, he put his front paws into her arms when she bent down as if he knew that his exam was about to take place.

"It's like a lump. I think it's an abscess?"

I immediately started to feel guilty. An abscess would explain everything she'd described. It would also be a legit medical problem that I would definitely want to see before a three-day hurricane weekend. When Melissa put him on the table, I immediately started looking over his back.

"Right here, can you see it?" Mrs. Esposito asked as she spread the hairs on JJ's right hip. I looked between her bright red fingernails and failed to see what she was referring to.

"I'm not seeing it. Is it like a swelling?" I asked as I started to look beyond the area she was focused on. I even ran my own hand around his back and hips looking for an obvious swelling.

"The red swollen area. See it? Look real close," she instructed.

My eyes finally caught sight of a small, red raised portion of his skin, less than half a centimeter in diameter.

"You mean this?" I asked.

"Yes! That's it. That's exactly it! Is that the start of an abscess? I read all about it online. I wanted to get him here and on antibiotics before it got any bigger. I know it's bothering him because that's the exact area he's been scratching," she replied, sounding relieved I had found it.

"The good news is that's not an abscess—" I stopped because in my mind the bad-news side of the story, was that it was fleas. Which, really, is bad news for me. When it comes to fleas and more specifically, flea prevention, she has her own set of beliefs. It had been an ongoing issue with her, and her record was filled with skin appointments that could have been avoided if she had used proper flea prevention. There was no way I was going to get into all that with her again. At least not at five o'clock, on a Friday, before a three-day hurricane weekend. So, I had to avoid that sensitive subject.

"It's what we call a papule. It's basically a small inflamed area—" I said, rushing to finish up his exam.

"Is that the precursor of an abscess?" she asked, interrupting me.

"No, it's just a localized area of inflammation from him scratching The rest of his skin is normal, so I think we just need to address his itching for now. I'd like to give him a short-acting steroid injection, to make him more comfortable. Then you can start him on some antihistamines—"

I was interrupted again but this time by Melissa. She may not have had the complete low down on Mrs. Esposito but she had been in veterinary medicine long enough to know it was time to try and bail on this five o'clock special. With a move that would have made Jen proud, she stated, "Dr. Miller, why don't you go ahead and grab JJ's shot while I'm still holding him. I know he'd probably like to get that part all over with. Right, buddy?" she said as she rubbed his head.

I excused myself and drew up his injection. I was gone less than a minute but when I returned Mrs. Esposito had turned the page on the little yellow notepad. She had also produced a pen and was making notes when I walked in.

"Dr. Millah, I have a couple of questions. You are giving him something for itching but what about the swelling? Shouldn't we start him on antibiotics, so it doesn't become an abscess? What caused him to itch in the first place?" she asked, looking up from her notepad and poised to make more notes with her pen. It felt like I was being interviewed by a police detective.

"It's not going to become an abscess. It's just a very small, localized area of inflammation. Really, his skin is normal, as was the rest of his exam. I'm just treating his itching. If he keeps itching, he might irritate his skin enough that it could become infected. As to what's causing his itching… It's most likely allergies…" I said, omitting that it was most likely fleas that he was allergic to.

After I gave him his injection, Melissa placed JJ on the floor. Mrs. Esposito took a long pause and looked at her notepad. It felt like minutes. I braced myself for the next question, anticipating she would make the connection and ask what it was that he was allergic to.

"Well… that makes sense. Thank Gawd I was able to get him here before that storm. Sometimes I wish I was still in New York. I hate these hurricanes. I'm just so happy he is going to be OK." Visibly relieved, and borderline excited, she couldn't contain herself. She caught Melissa off guard and gave her an awkward sideways hug. She wasn't the only one who was relieved.

"Let's go, JJ. After all this, Mommy needs to lie down. Thanks, Dr. Millah. Come on, baby, let's go get a treat from Liz. She owes you one after that shot." And with that, she was gone. But she'd be back. Oh boy, would she be back. But that wasn't until after the hurricane.

Darkness

The hurricane arrived early Monday morning, just as they said it would. When the feeder bands hit my house Sunday night, my wife and both my kids were glued to the local weatherman on TV. He was explaining a map of our area, littered with spinning icons. The icons represented tornados associated with the hurricane's feeder bands. Just as he pointed to the one that appeared to be traveling right toward us, in dramatic fashion, we lost all our power. The hurricane had officially arrived.

Make no mistake, hurricanes are serious business, and this one, in particular, wreaked havoc, destruction, and caused loss of life before it reached us. It can be a scary thing to live through, particularly when it's large and lingering like that one was. It lasted over six hours. The wind and rain were relentless. The loud gusts of wind pounding against our windows gave the impression that they'd blow out any minute. Each gust made me wish that I had renewed my membership in the boarding group.

Anticipating damage at home and at work, was no picnic. It was a long night. In both cases, I was blessed, and the damage was minimal. We also didn't get hit by any tornados. Most notably, the one that was swirling close by when the TV cut out. But less than a mile from my house, several giant oak trees had been ripped out, and a few homes had their pool screens completely crushed. No doubt, damage from a tornado. The only issue that I thought I would have to deal with was a loss of power. However, there were a few other minor issues that week and, of course, one major one.

Tuesday 8:22 am

One thing is for sure, I'm a creature of habit. With no power at home, and nothing else to entertain myself with, I figured I might as well make an early start of checking on the practice. Even though it was a perfectly sunny day, the downed trees, scattered debris, and sporadic property damage made it clear that a serious storm had just passed through. No one was going to work that day and the roads were deserted. Without any traffic, I made it to work ten minutes early. I was quite proud of myself for actually even showing up. My celebration was short-lived because my staff were all already there.

They were all in the parking lot working hard to clear debris. Looking at the pile of branches and leaves accumulating in the dumpster, it was apparent that they had been working for some time. It was an obvious reminder of how great my staff really are. Needless to say, it took all the joy out of my early arrival.

"Don't worry, Dr. Miller, us *girls* are getting all the hard work done, as usual. Everything OK at your house?" Jen caught me, as soon as I got out of my car.

"Yeah, some shingles blew off and a lot of debris. But we got pretty lucky. No power but, that's a given. How about you guys?" I replied.

"Nothing. We got it all locked down at my house. You know I'm like a survival prepper. So, I'm all set. We can go for days. I keep telling you, you need to get a generator like me. Especially for here." As always, Jen was the first to answer. Everyone else checked in with the same report; no damage, but their power was also gone.

"What's the news inside?" I reluctantly asked as I motioned toward the practice.

"Looks like you got really lucky for the most part," Jen replied, as she put a large pile of leaves in the dumpster.

"Most part?" I asked, already starting to fear my luck had run out.

"Well, it looks like there was a leak under the back wall in the back-kennel area. And the carpet in our office got a little wet. Well, actually… it got soaked by the side door. The storm must have blown rain under the gap from outside. How long have I been telling you to get that fixed? And let me warn you, it is already starting to smell like mildew…"

I immediately went inside and did a walkthrough. I couldn't find anything else. The leak in the kennel had come under the wall from the outside. The water had already been cleaned up but I could see a five-foot-long stain along the bottom of the wall.

When I checked our office, Jen had already put towels down to try and absorb the water. Without any air conditioning, the office was already starting to feel like a sauna. The mildew smell, she had warned me about, was overpowering. I knew I would have to make my first phone call from outside.

As with all storms, my first order of business was to call the power and the phone companies. My track record for getting our stuff back on early is stellar. Whenever I celebrate this fact, Liz is quick to correct me. According to her, the reason our power is always restored so quickly has to do with the fact that our practice shares the grid with the local courthouse and associated jail. She never gives me any credit for my ability to handle these companies in short order, and get our practice bumped up on their list.

It took me ten minutes to verbally push and shove my way up the customer service food chain at the power company. Finally, I reached the supervisor, and after wearing her down, she promised to put me on the priority list. It was just then when a familiar car pulled into the parking lot. It seemed her arrival was purposely slow and deliberate, in order to make it more dramatic. The driver's door slowly opened, and seconds later the iconic three-pronged cane, ever-so-slowly landed on the asphalt.

As she slowly stood up, she belted out, "Thank goodness you're all here! I was wondering whether or not to come for my appointment. Nobody bothered to call me! I'm here for her vaccines. Who knows what kind of disease we're going to be seeing 'cause of that hurricane." As if on cue, her white poodle, Cuddles, jumped down out of the car.

It was Mrs. Sweet. Liz had called her numerous times on Friday, and it was no surprise she never managed to get a hold of her. Mrs. Sweet has an answering machine but leaving a message on it is a complete waste of time. She either doesn't check it or never really figured out how to use it. For all the years she's had it, it still has the generic electronic greeting voice that came with it.

"Boy, you guys did a great job clearing this lot. I hope Dr. Miller appreciates the employees he's got here. I can see *he's* working really hard over there," she said, pointing to me across the parking lot with her cane. When she made it to the front door she paused. Cuddles, who was all too familiar with this drill, sat down at the end of her leash.

"Oh, let me get that for you. Cassey brought back a few things in a cooler, just in case. We should be able to do her annual today. I'll check," Liz explained, as she held open the door. As usual, Liz lived up to her role as a people pleaser and dismissed the opportunity to reschedule her. When my last hope, that Cassey hadn't brought any vaccines vanished, it was apparent that I was doing that annual.

That day, Mrs. Sweet was wearing a bright red T-shirt with a silhouette of a poodle, and "Keep Calm and Poodle on" printed below it. She was also sporting the classic white, almost translucent, pants that seem to be a staple item in the wardrobe of most all my older clients. Liz grabbed the record, Cassey grabbed a little muzzle, and the annual was underway.

Don't let that name fool you; Cuddles can be nasty. Don't laugh, it's true. For that reason alone, she always has to wear a muzzle in our practice. On that visit, however, she was quite well-behaved. She didn't once growl, cry out, or even try to bite me through the muzzle.

Mrs. Sweet dispensed her usual pleasantries and seemed genuinely relieved that my family, as well as Cassey's, were OK after the hurricane. After which, she wasted no time reminding us, more than once, on how hot and dark the exam room was.

Despite Mrs. Sweet's complaints, the exam proceeded without an issue, and the ambient light was more than sufficient. I was beginning to see things from Liz's point of view. Maybe helping Mrs. Sweet out and, better yet, getting this annual over with today wasn't such a bad idea after all. That thought was short-lived when a little problem came up at the end of her visit.

"Dr. Miller, I'm sorry sir. The distemper vaccine isn't in the cooler," Jen said, poking her head through the door, as she handed me a rabies vaccine. The look on Cassey's face was obvious. She was anxious to answer back but was restraining herself until after the annual. Mrs. Sweet was oblivious to what was going on. She didn't even notice me give Cuddles her rabies vaccine, never mind catch the news from Jen.

When I explained it to her, things didn't go over too well. She had a hard time grasping why we didn't have the vaccine after Liz had informed her we did. After which, she looked me straight in the eye, lifted her cane and pointed the handle at me for emphasis, and stated, "Doctor, let me tell you something: you have a practice here in Florida, and you know we have these storms. You should take the proper precautions and make a list of things to do to prepare. I know you are a busy man preparing for your home, family, and business, but this is something that you *must* take care of. Not just for me but for all your clients. The medication you have here is very precious." She paused intently, staring at me for added effect.

Cassey, anxious to go double check the cooler, took the muzzle off Cuddles and handed the leash to her. Mrs. Sweet then stood up and restarted.

"Thanks, dear. I guess we'll have to come back. Hopefully when the a/c and power are back on. I have to be honest with you, Doctor. It might have been a better idea to have rescheduled all this in the first place. When you get to be my age, it's quite an ordeal to go back and forth to the vet like this." Mrs. Sweet gave me one last disapproving look before she turned and left.

I went to the treatment area and found Jen and Cassey in the middle of a heated debate about the distemper vaccines. It had already been established that the distemper vaccine had been left behind in our freezer along with the other non-essential drugs. Making matters worse, the original list had now mysteriously vanished. Without it, it would be impossible to determine whether Cassey forgot them, or Jen had left them off the list to begin with.

As soon as she saw me, Jen immediately started. "I'm sorry, sir, the vaccines already felt kind of warm. I didn't want to chance it on Cuddles. I'm certain they were on the list. I can… I can only apologize. But don't worry, sir, I'll get on top of it. I'll talk with the manufacturer, they owe me one. It will be OK, sir. I promise."

Anytime Jen actually issues an apology and uses sir on top of it, I know the news isn't good. She knew as well as I do that this was all good in theory, however, with the current state of affairs, we had no idea when the manufacturer could get our stuff delivered. Not to mention that we wouldn't be able to schedule any dog annuals until we had that vaccine.

I wanted to vent, especially after I had just got lectured by, of all clients, Mrs. Sweet. But I restrained myself, regardless of who was responsible, I should have double checked it myself. And that point I couldn't overlook. "It doesn't matter who forgot what. Next time, maybe, how about you guys at least let me double check—"

"Yeah, yeah, sir. We hear you. I think we both got the message by now, OK? Let's just go finish up outside so we can all get out of here. Believe it or not, we could actually use your help out there," she said, cutting me off, and wasting no time playing *that* card.

We all made short work of clearing the remaining debris. Despite the fact that I cleared all the large branches, and the vaccines weren't in the cooler, Jen didn't let their hard work or early arrival go to waste. She used the opportunity to not only leverage that everyone could leave before noon but added that I was now in debt for yet another staff lunch. Since the emergency clinic was still open I agreed and decided to open at our scheduled time on Wednesday. Hoping by then that my phone skills would pay off and our power would be back on.

11:05 am

Jen and I were the last ones to leave. I left before Jen and was at the end of the street when a familiar black Cadillac passed me. I sat at the light waiting for it to change. I was prepared to do a U-turn and embrace my impending fate. Minutes felt like hours, and my mind was already trying to work out if this was going to be a legitimate medical issue. Just then my cell phone buzzed. It was a text and it was from Jen.

> *"Don't turn around! It's Esposito. It's not an emergency, trust me. Just keep going, I got it."*

The light changed, and at first, I was relieved. Then I started to overanalyze the situation. Had Jen actually spoken to Mrs. Esposito before she sent that text, or was she just trying to preemptively save me? The further I drove, the more I anticipated having to turn around. I decided to pull into a gas station until I heard back from Jen. I sat there parked and stared at all the pump handles covered with orange plastic bags. As with all hurricanes, this station had run out of gas, and

I had started to wonder when the supply would be replenished. It was then that my phone buzzed with my long-awaited text.

> *"Don't worry, sir. I handled it. JJ is fine. His skin is the same maybe slightly more irritated. She hasn't been giving the Benadryl like you told her. I told her the dose again, and to give him an oatmeal bath. You know what it is and you're going to have to address it with her. I told her to come first thing in the morning. Sorry but you better come on time. See you in the AM. Have a good one, sir!"*

Wednesday 8:20 am

The traffic was non-existent and I made it to work again in record time. When I arrived, I immediately noticed the door to our office was held open by a doorstop. Jen had also set up a box fan inside, and as soon as I approached the doorway I was immediately hit by the stench of mildew. It was slightly better inside but not by much. As I proceeded down the hallway and into the treatment area, I finally ditched the mildew smell and got a whiff of fresh cool air.

"Good morning, sir. Nice one! The power and phones are back on. But, as you can smell and see, there is a little bad news this morning," Jen said pointing to the exam-room door that had an all-too-familiar chart waiting for me.

"How are you guys doing? I still got no power—"

She cut me off and she grabbed the chart and continued, "Yeah, we know. No one's got power. OK. Just be lucky we got it here. Let's go, Dr. Miller. It's self-check-in and I'd like to get this over with…" As she opened the exam-room door her attitude immediately changed.

"Good morning, Mrs. Esposito! How are you doing this morning?"

"Not good. JJ was itching all night. He's just miserable. Nothing is working. Then, on top of all that we still got no power. I just know the heat is making him worse. Thank Gawd you guys are here today. I don't think I could go through all this another night."

206

I instinctively walked through the door behind Jen and she handed me the chart. She took JJ from Mrs. Esposito's arms. On that day, Mrs. Esposito was wearing a burgundy, velour tracksuit, her white visor, and flip-flops. The yellow notepad was already out in her other hand.

"We still have no power at my house either. This hurricane was pretty rough. We all might be in the dark for a while on this one," I replied, as I examined JJ. His only abnormality was the skin along his hind end that was bright red. I already knew what was wrong with him. And as always, I dove straight in; "I feel sorry for JJ as it's not easy being part Jack Russell here in Florida. His relatives are notorious for having allergies. Especially to…"

Fleas!

I'd guestimate that over eighty percent of the dermatology cases we see in our practice are caused by fleas. Regardless, if it's a little itching or a severe skin infection, fleas are going to be involved. Diagnosing and treating these conditions is easy. The problem lies in convincing my clients. Whether they think I'm trying to sell them flea prevention or they're just holding out for a more exciting diagnosis like allergies, they don't want to believe me. And when it comes to living in denial about fleas, Mrs. Esposito took it to another level.

"Fleas, oh no, not JJ. We got *the tag*. The one he's wearing, I just gawt that one."

'The Tag' she was referring to was a two-inch flat plastic tag that she'd got online and which hangs off JJ's collar. The company claims to use a combination of astrophysics and advanced computer technology (science that is so complicated that it can't be explained and an electromagnetic strip like on your credit card) to create a biomechanical force field to repel fleas off your pet.

"I have to tell you, Mrs. Esposito. You already know I'm not a big fan of that tag. If it worked as well as they claimed, don't you think the veterinary pharmaceutical companies would be using them?" I had been through all this before, on too many occasions. Her response was always the same.

"I know, I know, Dr. Miller, but we've tried all your flea stuff here. None of it works for him. All the flea pills you got make JJ sick. Then he gets tired for days. He's just not the same on those pills. You also know he can't take that stuff you put on his back either, 'cause of his surgery and everything. Not to mention, I think that stuff burns him."

You can do the math on the validity of those claims, as well as the effectiveness of a plastic tag with a magnetic strip counting as effective flea prevention.

"Well, I'm really worried that JJ is highly allergic to fleas. That's why he's itching. The distribution on his back is classic. Unfortunately, the hurricane we just had is going to mean even more flea—"

"I agree with you one hundred percent on the allergies. I just wish you could figure out what he's allergic to. I hear ya about the fleas and all that but we treat our property organically. If we had fleas I'd know it. Trust me," Mrs. Esposito replied, cutting me off, as she flipped over the top two pages on her yellow pad. Jen took that as her cue, placed JJ on the floor, and made her usual stealthy exit.

"I know you said allergies last time, and I've been looking into it. I have been reading a lot about all grain and stuff they put in dog food. I checked his, and it's got grain. I spoke to the breeder last week, and she doesn't have any of her dogs on grain. All they get is an all-natural holistic diet. You think we should try switching his food?" she asked, looking up from her pad and poised with her pen.

"Grain isn't an allergen, even for the dogs that truly have food allergies. It's definitely possible that he has allergies to things in his environment. But food, at this point, is a lot lower on the list."

"You said things in his environment. Like what? If you could tell me that, I'd get rid of it. What could it be?" she asked again, scribbling something on her pad.

"Much of treating allergies has to do with suppressing the response, rather than eliminating the cause. Even when dermatologists do allergy testing, the goal is to desensitize patients to what they are allergic to, like allergy shots in people—"

"You think he needs allergy shots?" she said, flipping the page and feverishly writing on her pad.

"No. Well, he might. I do think, maybe going to see the dermatologist would be a good idea though. I think we have exhausted everything here, and I think we need to get to the bottom of his itching…"

She paused and looked down at her pad. JJ was lying next to her on the floor and seemed oblivious to what was going on. Her response caught me completely off guard.

"I think, I think you're right. We need to get to the bottom of these allergies. It kinda makes sense. Let's do it! I'll go," she blurted out and then made an additional note on her pad.

Luckily, not only were they open and seeing appointments, they had an opening for her on Friday. When I gave Mrs. Esposito the dermatologist's card, she wrote the appointment time on both the card and her yellow pad. She then enthusiastically thanked me and left.

I was in the treatment area, taking pride in writing on her record, "Referral to dermatologist for second opinion; suspect flea allergy." I had finally made the referral, which was overdue, and she had actually agreed.

My celebration was short-lived. Before I could even ask Jen if she wanted to bet on the diagnosis the dermatologist was going to hand out, she stood over me as I was writing and stated, "You think you're so slick, Dr. Miller, don't you? I can tell you right now, that's not going to work out like you think it is. One way or another she'll work her way back in here and we'll be back to square one again. Going round and round with her about fleas. I swear, sometimes this place is like some sort of vortex; a vortex of hell!"

As usual, I blew her off, thinking she was especially cranky after having no power at home and now having no place to relax since our office still stank of mildew. But this time I was wrong.

Thursday 8:58 am

I had just finished my appointment with Mr. Deny. Like many of our clients after the hurricane, he was battling fleas. Unlike at his many previous appointments, Mr. Deny offered little resistance to my diagnosis and recommendations. Probably because on that appointment, his cat Johnny Cash was covered in fleas, and his skin was a mess. He was uncharacteristically receptive to all my medical advice. But as he left he did manage to get in a parting shot saying, "The last time I was robbed that bad I was still living in Detroit!"

When I came out of the exam room, her chart was waiting for me in my call box. There was a pink slip in Liz's handwriting: *Mrs. Esposito, call back regarding derm appointment on Friday. She wants to discuss other options. Requested recheck appointment for Friday morning here instead. Call ASAP.*

That call didn't go as planned. After I hung up, Mrs. Esposito immediately called back and told Liz she wasn't going to be coming back to see 'that Dr. Miller' ever again and to immediately fax all her records to Dr. David Macintosh. He was going to see her Friday afternoon since I refused to see her and denied access to care for her precious JJ. If that wasn't enough, she ended the call with a rhetorical question for Liz asking, "How could you possibly continue to work for such a disingenuous veterinarian?"

I'll explain it to you, just like I explained it to everyone else that day. When I called her back, it was like she had a prepared speech and had been waiting to give it to me. Mrs. Esposito informed me that she'd thought long and hard about it, and it was too far for her to drive to the dermatologist. I tried to explain that the dermatologist is actually closer than the neurologist she'd taken JJ to. She wanted no part of it. Her mind was made up. She was also adamant that I see her again, as my first appointment Friday morning.

After she finally finished, I told her that JJ had had this problem for a long time and I even quoted from his record, all the dates he'd come to see me for his skin. I went on to tell her that I could see and treat JJ but he would only end up coming back. The dermatologist, on the other hand, would be able to get to the root of his potential allergies and find a long-term solution, just like she herself had agreed with yesterday. Finally, I confessed to her that his referral was overdue, and I should have done it sooner.

I felt my argument was pretty compelling and well presented. It was exactly what was needed to bring her back from the dark side. Unfortunately, it produced a response that I hadn't anticipated.

"If you don't want to see JJ anymore, that's fine, Dr. Millah! I already have someone who will!" she exclaimed and abruptly hung up.

After I explained it all to Jen, she was visibly upset and wasted no time voicing her opinion.

"What did I tell you, Dr. Miller? I knew she wasn't going to go to the dermatologist. I knew it. But to go to another vet? I'm actually disappointed. After all the years we invested in her, that's the way we get treated. Good luck with Dr. Macintosh. I'm not missing dealing with that. But really, I am going to miss JJ. I just pray that eventually, he gets the *real* vet care somewhere because I know Dr. Macintosh isn't going to fix that, especially with her. And, oh yeah, I want that record. Liz needs to know if she ever calls, trying to get back in here, after all we did for her, after what she said, *I personally* want to talk to her."

As it turned out, all our prayers were answered. Not only did JJ get the proper care but, in a weird turn of events, we were directly notified about it, three weeks later.

Epilogue

I tried using the same phone skills to turn the power back on at my house. Despite multiple phone calls and supervisors, I didn't manage to get the miracle I was looking for. I was in the dark for well over three days. But I was the first one in our practice to get their power back on. Cassey, on the other hand, was one of the last ones to get hers on. I offered to call the power company on her behalf more than once. I even guaranteed my success when she told me she had a power line down in the street on her block. She turned me down every time and it would be eight days before she finally got hers back. Despite my stellar track record with the practice, and my above average record at home, Liz and even Cassey will tell you my calling these people has nothing to do with getting my power on.

The leak in the kennel area turned out later to be an inexpensive fix. It involved a little extra concrete along the foundation. I'm no handyman and Liz's cousin had to handle that job. Unlike the kennel leak, the office turned out to be a lot more involved than we'd initially thought.

After two weeks, and three trips by a carpet-cleaning company (whose name I won't mention but it sounds a lot like steamer), it still stunk in our office. Jen finally took matters into her own hands and did what she does best: went on her phone to research it online. I lost all hope once I saw her 'great' solution was to spray vinegar, apply baking soda, and then vacuum the area. She did it religiously for three days and, lo and behold, it actually worked. She then made me apologize and claims I still owe her lunch for my complete lack of faith and because she saved me from having to pay to have the carpet replaced. For the record, Jen and Liz also wanted me to make it clear that the door has not been fixed.

It's still highly contested as to whether the vaccines were left off Jen's list or if Cassey had forgotten to take them. Jen did make good with her promise, and we did get a free tray of vaccines from the manufacturer. I never told them but I eventually found that original list. I found it under a stack of women's fitness magazines in the break room. Before you ask why I was rummaging through women's magazines in the first place, the more important point is that the vaccines weren't on that list.

I was going to confront Jen, especially after all the grief she gives me every time I go to double check on her. But, I changed my mind and ripped it up. I'd like to tell you I threw it out to let her slide but I'm not one of *those* practice owners. Every so often, when the time is right or I need to get out of a sticky situation, I'll bring up those vaccines again. I'll let her and Cassey try to figure it out on their own. Which is still always entertaining.

Three weeks later, when no one was paying attention or expecting it, a fax came in after hours. It was a report from the dermatologist for JJ Esposito. Dr. Macintosh was listed as her primary vet on the report. But they mistakenly also faxed it to us. Most likely since I had set up that original referral. It appeared that Dr. Macintosh played around with the case for a few weeks before JJ finally ended up at the dermatologist. We aren't too sure which one of them made that decision but, according to the report, by the time that they saw JJ, his skin already had a pretty nasty secondary infection. Their reported diagnosis: *FAD. (flea allergy dermatitis).* As I expected, they had more success in getting her to give JJ proper flea prevention. Well, at least she took it, according to the report.

As far as we know, Ann Marie Esposito still sees Dr. Macintosh. For now, the 'Esposito, Ann Marie' record is still buried under a stack of papers on Jen's desk. It sits, awaiting that call, whenever it comes. There was another New York client shortly after Esposito's exodus. So soon, that Jen labeled it a 'great client trade.' As with all our stories, that trade wasn't as 'great' as Jen made it out to be.

It didn't matter that Jen initially called Mr. Rossi one of her new favorite clients, or that she was all excited because he was also from the Bronx, just like her. When things didn't work out as well as she thought they would, she was quick to re-assign him as yet another one of *my* favorite New York clients.

Jen and the staff used their usual, tired excuses, claiming that proofreading a chapter about Mr. Rossi would give them all stress-associated GI issues. For Jen, there is a little more to the story than just that. Nonetheless, I had to promise not to include that story here. Don't worry, I've just started working on them about that. Despite what you may think, I still run this show. You didn't think I actually kept that Beyoncé ring tone, did you? Trust me, they'll all cave eventually, even Jen.